C-2864   CAREER EXAMINATION SERIES

This is your
PASSBOOK for...

Librarian Trainee

Test Preparation Study Guide
Questions & Answers

NATIONAL LEARNING CORPORATION®

COPYRIGHT NOTICE

This book is SOLELY intended for, is sold ONLY to, and its use is RESTRICTED to individual, bona fide applicants or candidates who qualify by virtue of having seriously filed applications for appropriate license, certificate, professional and/or promotional advancement, higher school matriculation, scholarship, or other legitimate requirements of education and/or governmental authorities.

This book is NOT intended for use, class instruction, tutoring, training, duplication, copying, reprinting, excerption, or adaptation, etc., by:

1) Other publishers
2) Proprietors and/or Instructors of "Coaching" and/or Preparatory Courses
3) Personnel and/or Training Divisions of commercial, industrial, and governmental organizations
4) Schools, colleges, or universities and/or their departments and staffs, including teachers and other personnel
5) Testing Agencies or Bureaus
6) Study groups which seek by the purchase of a single volume to copy and/or duplicate and/or adapt this material for use by the group as a whole without having purchased individual volumes for each of the members of the group
7) Et al.

Such persons would be in violation of appropriate Federal and State statutes.

PROVISION OF LICENSING AGREEMENTS – Recognized educational, commercial, industrial, and governmental institutions and organizations, and others legitimately engaged in educational pursuits, including training, testing, and measurement activities, may address request for a licensing agreement to the copyright owners, who will determine whether, and under what conditions, including fees and charges, the materials in this book may be used them. In other words, a licensing facility exists for the legitimate use of the material in this book on other than an individual basis. However, it is asseverated and affirmed here that the material in this book CANNOT be used without the receipt of the express permission of such a licensing agreement from the Publishers. Inquiries re licensing should be addressed to the company, attention rights and permissions department.

All rights reserved, including the right of reproduction in whole or in part, in any form or by any means, electronic or mechanical, including photocopying, recording, or by any information storage and retrieval system, without permission in writing from the Publisher.

Copyright © 2024 by
National Learning Corporation

212 Michael Drive, Syosset, NY 11791
(516) 921-8888 • www.passbooks.com
E-mail: info@passbooks.com

PUBLISHED IN THE UNITED STATES OF AMERICA

PASSBOOK® SERIES

THE *PASSBOOK® SERIES* has been created to prepare applicants and candidates for the ultimate academic battlefield – the examination room.

At some time in our lives, each and every one of us may be required to take an examination – for validation, matriculation, admission, qualification, registration, certification, or licensure.

Based on the assumption that every applicant or candidate has met the basic formal educational standards, has taken the required number of courses, and read the necessary texts, the *PASSBOOK® SERIES* furnishes the one special preparation which may assure passing with confidence, instead of failing with insecurity. Examination questions – together with answers – are furnished as the basic vehicle for study so that the mysteries of the examination and its compounding difficulties may be eliminated or diminished by a sure method.

This book is meant to help you pass your examination provided that you qualify and are serious in your objective.

The entire field is reviewed through the huge store of content information which is succinctly presented through a provocative and challenging approach – the question-and-answer method.

A climate of success is established by furnishing the correct answers at the end of each test.

You soon learn to recognize types of questions, forms of questions, and patterns of questioning. You may even begin to anticipate expected outcomes.

You perceive that many questions are repeated or adapted so that you can gain acute insights, which may enable you to score many sure points.

You learn how to confront new questions, or types of questions, and to attack them confidently and work out the correct answers.

You note objectives and emphases, and recognize pitfalls and dangers, so that you may make positive educational adjustments.

Moreover, you are kept fully informed in relation to new concepts, methods, practices, and directions in the field.

You discover that you are actually taking the examination all the time: you are preparing for the examination by "taking" an examination, not by reading extraneous and/or supererogatory textbooks.

In short, this PASSBOOK®, used directedly, should be an important factor in helping you to pass your test.

LIBRARIAN TRAINEE

DUTIES
Works under the supervision and guidance of a professional librarian, learning library procedures, techniques and skills in all areas of library science while attending an accredited library school. Pursues a graduate program leading to a master's degree in librarianship. Librarian Trainees may be assigned increased professional responsibilities and some supervisory responsibilities over the work of nonprofessional employees for particular assignments. Does related work as required.

EXAMPLES OF TYPICAL TASKS
Provides advisory and guidance services to library users; performs original cataloging and classification techniques; answers reference questions for the public and library staff; assists in collection development, recommending titles for purchase and/or deletion; performs online computer searches of database; provides training on conduct of online searching to users; compiles bibliographies; conducts tours, book talks, multi-media programs, story and picture book hours; instructs the public in the use of library resources; supervises the work of clerical, paraprofessional and volunteer personnel for particular assignments; keeps informed of professional developments.

SCOPE OF THE EXAMINATION
The <u>written test</u> will cover knowledge, skills and/or abilities in such areas as:

1. Information technology and the library;
2. Logic;
3. Library resources and practices; and
4. Librarian/patron relations.

HOW TO TAKE A TEST

I. YOU MUST PASS AN EXAMINATION

A. WHAT EVERY CANDIDATE SHOULD KNOW

Examination applicants often ask us for help in preparing for the written test. What can I study in advance? What kinds of questions will be asked? How will the test be given? How will the papers be graded?

As an applicant for a civil service examination, you may be wondering about some of these things. Our purpose here is to suggest effective methods of advance study and to describe civil service examinations.

Your chances for success on this examination can be increased if you know how to prepare. Those "pre-examination jitters" can be reduced if you know what to expect. You can even experience an adventure in good citizenship if you know why civil service exams are given.

B. WHY ARE CIVIL SERVICE EXAMINATIONS GIVEN?

Civil service examinations are important to you in two ways. As a citizen, you want public jobs filled by employees who know how to do their work. As a job seeker, you want a fair chance to compete for that job on an equal footing with other candidates. The best-known means of accomplishing this two-fold goal is the competitive examination.

Exams are widely publicized throughout the nation. They may be administered for jobs in federal, state, city, municipal, town or village governments or agencies.

Any citizen may apply, with some limitations, such as the age or residence of applicants. Your experience and education may be reviewed to see whether you meet the requirements for the particular examination. When these requirements exist, they are reasonable and applied consistently to all applicants. Thus, a competitive examination may cause you some uneasiness now, but it is your privilege and safeguard.

C. HOW ARE CIVIL SERVICE EXAMS DEVELOPED?

Examinations are carefully written by trained technicians who are specialists in the field known as "psychological measurement," in consultation with recognized authorities in the field of work that the test will cover. These experts recommend the subject matter areas or skills to be tested; only those knowledges or skills important to your success on the job are included. The most reliable books and source materials available are used as references. Together, the experts and technicians judge the difficulty level of the questions.

Test technicians know how to phrase questions so that the problem is clearly stated. Their ethics do not permit "trick" or "catch" questions. Questions may have been tried out on sample groups, or subjected to statistical analysis, to determine their usefulness.

Written tests are often used in combination with performance tests, ratings of training and experience, and oral interviews. All of these measures combine to form the best-known means of finding the right person for the right job.

II. HOW TO PASS THE WRITTEN TEST

A. NATURE OF THE EXAMINATION

To prepare intelligently for civil service examinations, you should know how they differ from school examinations you have taken. In school you were assigned certain definite pages to read or subjects to cover. The examination questions were quite detailed and usually emphasized memory. Civil service exams, on the other hand, try to discover your present ability to perform the duties of a position, plus your potentiality to learn these duties. In other words, a civil service exam attempts to predict how successful you will be. Questions cover such a broad area that they cannot be as minute and detailed as school exam questions.

In the public service similar kinds of work, or positions, are grouped together in one "class." This process is known as *position-classification*. All the positions in a class are paid according to the salary range for that class. One class title covers all of these positions, and they are all tested by the same examination.

B. FOUR BASIC STEPS

1) Study the announcement

How, then, can you know what subjects to study? Our best answer is: "Learn as much as possible about the class of positions for which you've applied." The exam will test the knowledge, skills and abilities needed to do the work.

Your most valuable source of information about the position you want is the official exam announcement. This announcement lists the training and experience qualifications. Check these standards and apply only if you come reasonably close to meeting them.

The brief description of the position in the examination announcement offers some clues to the subjects which will be tested. Think about the job itself. Review the duties in your mind. Can you perform them, or are there some in which you are rusty? Fill in the blank spots in your preparation.

Many jurisdictions preview the written test in the exam announcement by including a section called "Knowledge and Abilities Required," "Scope of the Examination," or some similar heading. Here you will find out specifically what fields will be tested.

2) Review your own background

Once you learn in general what the position is all about, and what you need to know to do the work, ask yourself which subjects you already know fairly well and which need improvement. You may wonder whether to concentrate on improving your strong areas or on building some background in your fields of weakness. When the announcement has specified "some knowledge" or "considerable knowledge," or has used adjectives like "beginning principles of…" or "advanced … methods," you can get a clue as to the number and difficulty of questions to be asked in any given field. More questions, and hence broader coverage, would be included for those subjects which are more important in the work. Now weigh your strengths and weaknesses against the job requirements and prepare accordingly.

3) Determine the level of the position

Another way to tell how intensively you should prepare is to understand the level of the job for which you are applying. Is it the entering level? In other words, is this the position in which beginners in a field of work are hired? Or is it an intermediate or advanced level? Sometimes this is indicated by such words as "Junior" or "Senior" in the class title. Other jurisdictions use Roman numerals to designate the level – Clerk I, Clerk II, for example. The word "Supervisor" sometimes appears in the title. If the level is not indicated by the title, check the description of duties. Will you be working under very close supervision, or will you have responsibility for independent decisions in this work?

4) Choose appropriate study materials

Now that you know the subjects to be examined and the relative amount of each subject to be covered, you can choose suitable study materials. For beginning level jobs, or even advanced ones, if you have a pronounced weakness in some aspect of your training, read a modern, standard textbook in that field. Be sure it is up to date and has general coverage. Such books are normally available at your library, and the librarian will be glad to help you locate one. For entry-level positions, questions of appropriate difficulty are chosen – neither highly advanced questions, nor those too simple. Such questions require careful thought but not advanced training.

If the position for which you are applying is technical or advanced, you will read more advanced, specialized material. If you are already familiar with the basic principles of your field, elementary textbooks would waste your time. Concentrate on advanced textbooks and technical periodicals. Think through the concepts and review difficult problems in your field.

These are all general sources. You can get more ideas on your own initiative, following these leads. For example, training manuals and publications of the government agency which employs workers in your field can be useful, particularly for technical and professional positions. A letter or visit to the government department involved may result in more specific study suggestions, and certainly will provide you with a more definite idea of the exact nature of the position you are seeking.

III. KINDS OF TESTS

Tests are used for purposes other than measuring knowledge and ability to perform specified duties. For some positions, it is equally important to test ability to make adjustments to new situations or to profit from training. In others, basic mental abilities not dependent on information are essential. Questions which test these things may not appear as pertinent to the duties of the position as those which test for knowledge and information. Yet they are often highly important parts of a fair examination. For very general questions, it is almost impossible to help you direct your study efforts. What we can do is to point out some of the more common of these general abilities needed in public service positions and describe some typical questions.

1) General information

Broad, general information has been found useful for predicting job success in some kinds of work. This is tested in a variety of ways, from vocabulary lists to questions about current events. Basic background in some field of work, such as sociology or economics, may be sampled in a group of questions. Often these are principles which have become familiar to most persons through exposure rather than through formal training. It is difficult to advise you how to study for these questions; being alert to the world around you is our best suggestion.

2) Verbal ability

An example of an ability needed in many positions is verbal or language ability. Verbal ability is, in brief, the ability to use and understand words. Vocabulary and grammar tests are typical measures of this ability. Reading comprehension or paragraph interpretation questions are common in many kinds of civil service tests. You are given a paragraph of written material and asked to find its central meaning.

3) Numerical ability

Number skills can be tested by the familiar arithmetic problem, by checking paired lists of numbers to see which are alike and which are different, or by interpreting charts and graphs. In the latter test, a graph may be printed in the test booklet which you are asked to use as the basis for answering questions.

4) Observation

A popular test for law-enforcement positions is the observation test. A picture is shown to you for several minutes, then taken away. Questions about the picture test your ability to observe both details and larger elements.

5) Following directions

In many positions in the public service, the employee must be able to carry out written instructions dependably and accurately. You may be given a chart with several columns, each column listing a variety of information. The questions require you to carry out directions involving the information given in the chart.

6) Skills and aptitudes

Performance tests effectively measure some manual skills and aptitudes. When the skill is one in which you are trained, such as typing or shorthand, you can practice. These tests are often very much like those given in business school or high school courses. For many of the other skills and aptitudes, however, no short-time preparation can be made. Skills and abilities natural to you or that you have developed throughout your lifetime are being tested.

Many of the general questions just described provide all the data needed to answer the questions and ask you to use your reasoning ability to find the answers. Your best preparation for these tests, as well as for tests of facts and ideas, is to be at your physical and mental best. You, no doubt, have your own methods of getting into an exam-taking mood and keeping "in shape." The next section lists some ideas on this subject.

IV. KINDS OF QUESTIONS

Only rarely is the "essay" question, which you answer in narrative form, used in civil service tests. Civil service tests are usually of the short-answer type. Full instructions for answering these questions will be given to you at the examination. But in case this is your first experience with short-answer questions and separate answer sheets, here is what you need to know:

1) Multiple-choice Questions

Most popular of the short-answer questions is the "multiple choice" or "best answer" question. It can be used, for example, to test for factual knowledge, ability to solve problems or judgment in meeting situations found at work.

A multiple-choice question is normally one of three types—
- It can begin with an incomplete statement followed by several possible endings. You are to find the one ending which *best* completes the statement, although some of the others may not be entirely wrong.
- It can also be a complete statement in the form of a question which is answered by choosing one of the statements listed.

- It can be in the form of a problem – again you select the best answer.

Here is an example of a multiple-choice question with a discussion which should give you some clues as to the method for choosing the right answer:

When an employee has a complaint about his assignment, the action which will *best* help him overcome his difficulty is to
   A. discuss his difficulty with his coworkers
   B. take the problem to the head of the organization
   C. take the problem to the person who gave him the assignment
   D. say nothing to anyone about his complaint

In answering this question, you should study each of the choices to find which is best. Consider choice "A" – Certainly an employee may discuss his complaint with fellow employees, but no change or improvement can result, and the complaint remains unresolved. Choice "B" is a poor choice since the head of the organization probably does not know what assignment you have been given, and taking your problem to him is known as "going over the head" of the supervisor. The supervisor, or person who made the assignment, is the person who can clarify it or correct any injustice. Choice "C" is, therefore, correct. To say nothing, as in choice "D," is unwise. Supervisors have and interest in knowing the problems employees are facing, and the employee is seeking a solution to his problem.

2) True/False Questions

The "true/false" or "right/wrong" form of question is sometimes used. Here a complete statement is given. Your job is to decide whether the statement is right or wrong.

SAMPLE: A roaming cell-phone call to a nearby city costs less than a non-roaming call to a distant city.

This statement is wrong, or false, since roaming calls are more expensive.

This is not a complete list of all possible question forms, although most of the others are variations of these common types. You will always get complete directions for answering questions. Be sure you understand *how* to mark your answers – ask questions until you do.

V. RECORDING YOUR ANSWERS

Computer terminals are used more and more today for many different kinds of exams.

For an examination with very few applicants, you may be told to record your answers in the test booklet itself. Separate answer sheets are much more common. If this separate answer sheet is to be scored by machine – and this is often the case – it is highly important that you mark your answers correctly in order to get credit.

An electronic scoring machine is often used in civil service offices because of the speed with which papers can be scored. Machine-scored answer sheets must be marked with a pencil, which will be given to you. This pencil has a high graphite content which responds to the electronic scoring machine. As a matter of fact, stray dots may register as answers, so do not let your pencil rest on the answer sheet while you are pondering the correct answer. Also, if your pencil lead breaks or is otherwise defective, ask for another.

Since the answer sheet will be dropped in a slot in the scoring machine, be careful not to bend the corners or get the paper crumpled.

The answer sheet normally has five vertical columns of numbers, with 30 numbers to a column. These numbers correspond to the question numbers in your test booklet. After each number, going across the page are four or five pairs of dotted lines. These short dotted lines have small letters or numbers above them. The first two pairs may also have a "T" or "F" above the letters. This indicates that the first two pairs only are to be used if the questions are of the true-false type. If the questions are multiple choice, disregard the "T" and "F" and pay attention only to the small letters or numbers.

Answer your questions in the manner of the sample that follows:

32. The largest city in the United States is
    A. Washington, D.C.
    B. New York City
    C. Chicago
    D. Detroit
    E. San Francisco

1) Choose the answer you think is best. (New York City is the largest, so "B" is correct.)
2) Find the row of dotted lines numbered the same as the question you are answering. (Find row number 32)
3) Find the pair of dotted lines corresponding to the answer. (Find the pair of lines under the mark "B.")
4) Make a solid black mark between the dotted lines.

VI. BEFORE THE TEST

Common sense will help you find procedures to follow to get ready for an examination. Too many of us, however, overlook these sensible measures. Indeed, nervousness and fatigue have been found to be the most serious reasons why applicants fail to do their best on civil service tests. Here is a list of reminders:

- Begin your preparation early – Don't wait until the last minute to go scurrying around for books and materials or to find out what the position is all about.
- Prepare continuously – An hour a night for a week is better than an all-night cram session. This has been definitely established. What is more, a night a week for a month will return better dividends than crowding your study into a shorter period of time.
- Locate the place of the exam – You have been sent a notice telling you when and where to report for the examination. If the location is in a different town or otherwise unfamiliar to you, it would be well to inquire the best route and learn something about the building.
- Relax the night before the test – Allow your mind to rest. Do not study at all that night. Plan some mild recreation or diversion; then go to bed early and get a good night's sleep.
- Get up early enough to make a leisurely trip to the place for the test – This way unforeseen events, traffic snarls, unfamiliar buildings, etc. will not upset you.
- Dress comfortably – A written test is not a fashion show. You will be known by number and not by name, so wear something comfortable.

- Leave excess paraphernalia at home – Shopping bags and odd bundles will get in your way. You need bring only the items mentioned in the official notice you received; usually everything you need is provided. Do not bring reference books to the exam. They will only confuse those last minutes and be taken away from you when in the test room.
- Arrive somewhat ahead of time – If because of transportation schedules you must get there very early, bring a newspaper or magazine to take your mind off yourself while waiting.
- Locate the examination room – When you have found the proper room, you will be directed to the seat or part of the room where you will sit. Sometimes you are given a sheet of instructions to read while you are waiting. Do not fill out any forms until you are told to do so; just read them and be prepared.
- Relax and prepare to listen to the instructions
- If you have any physical problem that may keep you from doing your best, be sure to tell the test administrator. If you are sick or in poor health, you really cannot do your best on the exam. You can come back and take the test some other time.

VII. AT THE TEST

The day of the test is here and you have the test booklet in your hand. The temptation to get going is very strong. Caution! There is more to success than knowing the right answers. You must know how to identify your papers and understand variations in the type of short-answer question used in this particular examination. Follow these suggestions for maximum results from your efforts:

1) Cooperate with the monitor

The test administrator has a duty to create a situation in which you can be as much at ease as possible. He will give instructions, tell you when to begin, check to see that you are marking your answer sheet correctly, and so on. He is not there to guard you, although he will see that your competitors do not take unfair advantage. He wants to help you do your best.

2) Listen to all instructions

Don't jump the gun! Wait until you understand all directions. In most civil service tests you get more time than you need to answer the questions. So don't be in a hurry. Read each word of instructions until you clearly understand the meaning. Study the examples, listen to all announcements and follow directions. Ask questions if you do not understand what to do.

3) Identify your papers

Civil service exams are usually identified by number only. You will be assigned a number; you must not put your name on your test papers. Be sure to copy your number correctly. Since more than one exam may be given, copy your exact examination title.

4) Plan your time

Unless you are told that a test is a "speed" or "rate of work" test, speed itself is usually not important. Time enough to answer all the questions will be provided, but this does not mean that you have all day. An overall time limit has been set. Divide the total time (in minutes) by the number of questions to determine the approximate time you have for each question.

5) Do not linger over difficult questions

If you come across a difficult question, mark it with a paper clip (useful to have along) and come back to it when you have been through the booklet. One caution if you do this – be sure to skip a number on your answer sheet as well. Check often to be sure that you have not lost your place and that you are marking in the row numbered the same as the question you are answering.

6) Read the questions

Be sure you know what the question asks! Many capable people are unsuccessful because they failed to *read* the questions correctly.

7) Answer all questions

Unless you have been instructed that a penalty will be deducted for incorrect answers, it is better to guess than to omit a question.

8) Speed tests

It is often better NOT to guess on speed tests. It has been found that on timed tests people are tempted to spend the last few seconds before time is called in marking answers at random – without even reading them – in the hope of picking up a few extra points. To discourage this practice, the instructions may warn you that your score will be "corrected" for guessing. That is, a penalty will be applied. The incorrect answers will be deducted from the correct ones, or some other penalty formula will be used.

9) Review your answers

If you finish before time is called, go back to the questions you guessed or omitted to give them further thought. Review other answers if you have time.

10) Return your test materials

If you are ready to leave before others have finished or time is called, take ALL your materials to the monitor and leave quietly. Never take any test material with you. The monitor can discover whose papers are not complete, and taking a test booklet may be grounds for disqualification.

VIII. EXAMINATION TECHNIQUES

1) Read the general instructions carefully. These are usually printed on the first page of the exam booklet. As a rule, these instructions refer to the timing of the examination; the fact that you should not start work until the signal and must stop work at a signal, etc. If there are any *special* instructions, such as a choice of questions to be answered, make sure that you note this instruction carefully.

2) When you are ready to start work on the examination, that is as soon as the signal has been given, read the instructions to each question booklet, underline any key words or phrases, such as *least, best, outline, describe* and the like. In this way you will tend to answer as requested rather than discover on reviewing your paper that you *listed without describing*, that you selected the *worst* choice rather than the *best* choice, etc.

3) If the examination is of the objective or multiple-choice type – that is, each question will also give a series of possible answers: A, B, C or D, and you are called upon to select the best answer and write the letter next to that answer on your answer paper – it is advisable to start answering each question in turn. There may be anywhere from 50 to 100 such questions in the three or four hours allotted and you can see how much time would be taken if you read through all the questions before beginning to answer any. Furthermore, if you come across a question or group of questions which you know would be difficult to answer, it would undoubtedly affect your handling of all the other questions.

4) If the examination is of the essay type and contains but a few questions, it is a moot point as to whether you should read all the questions before starting to answer any one. Of course, if you are given a choice – say five out of seven and the like – then it is essential to read all the questions so you can eliminate the two that are most difficult. If, however, you are asked to answer all the questions, there may be danger in trying to answer the easiest one first because you may find that you will spend too much time on it. The best technique is to answer the first question, then proceed to the second, etc.

5) Time your answers. Before the exam begins, write down the time it started, then add the time allowed for the examination and write down the time it must be completed, then divide the time available somewhat as follows:
    - If 3-1/2 hours are allowed, that would be 210 minutes. If you have 80 objective-type questions, that would be an average of 2-1/2 minutes per question. Allow yourself no more than 2 minutes per question, or a total of 160 minutes, which will permit about 50 minutes to review.
    - If for the time allotment of 210 minutes there are 7 essay questions to answer, that would average about 30 minutes a question. Give yourself only 25 minutes per question so that you have about 35 minutes to review.

6) The most important instruction is to *read each question* and make sure you know what is wanted. The second most important instruction is to *time yourself properly* so that you answer every question. The third most important instruction is to *answer every question*. Guess if you have to but include something for each question. Remember that you will receive no credit for a blank and will probably receive some credit if you write something in answer to an essay question. If you guess a letter – say "B" for a multiple-choice question – you may have guessed right. If you leave a blank as an answer to a multiple-choice question, the examiners may respect your feelings but it will not add a point to your score. Some exams may penalize you for wrong answers, so in such cases *only*, you may not want to guess unless you have some basis for your answer.

7) Suggestions
    a. Objective-type questions
        1. Examine the question booklet for proper sequence of pages and questions
        2. Read all instructions carefully
        3. Skip any question which seems too difficult; return to it after all other questions have been answered
        4. Apportion your time properly; do not spend too much time on any single question or group of questions

5. Note and underline key words – *all, most, fewest, least, best, worst, same, opposite,* etc.
6. Pay particular attention to negatives
7. Note unusual option, e.g., unduly long, short, complex, different or similar in content to the body of the question
8. Observe the use of "hedging" words – *probably, may, most likely,* etc.
9. Make sure that your answer is put next to the same number as the question
10. Do not second-guess unless you have good reason to believe the second answer is definitely more correct
11. Cross out original answer if you decide another answer is more accurate; do not erase until you are ready to hand your paper in
12. Answer all questions; guess unless instructed otherwise
13. Leave time for review

   b. Essay questions
   1. Read each question carefully
   2. Determine exactly what is wanted. Underline key words or phrases.
   3. Decide on outline or paragraph answer
   4. Include many different points and elements unless asked to develop any one or two points or elements
   5. Show impartiality by giving pros and cons unless directed to select one side only
   6. Make and write down any assumptions you find necessary to answer the questions
   7. Watch your English, grammar, punctuation and choice of words
   8. Time your answers; don't crowd material

8) Answering the essay question

Most essay questions can be answered by framing the specific response around several key words or ideas. Here are a few such key words or ideas:

M's: manpower, materials, methods, money, management
P's: purpose, program, policy, plan, procedure, practice, problems, pitfalls, personnel, public relations

   a. Six basic steps in handling problems:
   1. Preliminary plan and background development
   2. Collect information, data and facts
   3. Analyze and interpret information, data and facts
   4. Analyze and develop solutions as well as make recommendations
   5. Prepare report and sell recommendations
   6. Install recommendations and follow up effectiveness

   b. Pitfalls to avoid
   1. *Taking things for granted* – A statement of the situation does not necessarily imply that each of the elements is necessarily true; for example, a complaint may be invalid and biased so that all that can be taken for granted is that a complaint has been registered

2. *Considering only one side of a situation* – Wherever possible, indicate several alternatives and then point out the reasons you selected the best one
3. *Failing to indicate follow up* – Whenever your answer indicates action on your part, make certain that you will take proper follow-up action to see how successful your recommendations, procedures or actions turn out to be
4. *Taking too long in answering any single question* – Remember to time your answers properly

IX. AFTER THE TEST

Scoring procedures differ in detail among civil service jurisdictions although the general principles are the same. Whether the papers are hand-scored or graded by machine we have described, they are nearly always graded by number. That is, the person who marks the paper knows only the number – never the name – of the applicant. Not until all the papers have been graded will they be matched with names. If other tests, such as training and experience or oral interview ratings have been given, scores will be combined. Different parts of the examination usually have different weights. For example, the written test might count 60 percent of the final grade, and a rating of training and experience 40 percent. In many jurisdictions, veterans will have a certain number of points added to their grades.

After the final grade has been determined, the names are placed in grade order and an eligible list is established. There are various methods for resolving ties between those who get the same final grade – probably the most common is to place first the name of the person whose application was received first. Job offers are made from the eligible list in the order the names appear on it. You will be notified of your grade and your rank as soon as all these computations have been made. This will be done as rapidly as possible.

People who are found to meet the requirements in the announcement are called "eligibles." Their names are put on a list of eligible candidates. An eligible's chances of getting a job depend on how high he stands on this list and how fast agencies are filling jobs from the list.

When a job is to be filled from a list of eligibles, the agency asks for the names of people on the list of eligibles for that job. When the civil service commission receives this request, it sends to the agency the names of the three people highest on this list. Or, if the job to be filled has specialized requirements, the office sends the agency the names of the top three persons who meet these requirements from the general list.

The appointing officer makes a choice from among the three people whose names were sent to him. If the selected person accepts the appointment, the names of the others are put back on the list to be considered for future openings.

That is the rule in hiring from all kinds of eligible lists, whether they are for typist, carpenter, chemist, or something else. For every vacancy, the appointing officer has his choice of any one of the top three eligibles on the list. This explains why the person whose name is on top of the list sometimes does not get an appointment when some of the persons lower on the list do. If the appointing officer chooses the second or third eligible, the No. 1 eligible does not get a job at once, but stays on the list until he is appointed or the list is terminated.

X. HOW TO PASS THE INTERVIEW TEST

The examination for which you applied requires an oral interview test. You have already taken the written test and you are now being called for the interview test – the final part of the formal examination.

You may think that it is not possible to prepare for an interview test and that there are no procedures to follow during an interview. Our purpose is to point out some things you can do in advance that will help you and some good rules to follow and pitfalls to avoid while you are being interviewed.

What is an interview supposed to test?

The written examination is designed to test the technical knowledge and competence of the candidate; the oral is designed to evaluate intangible qualities, not readily measured otherwise, and to establish a list showing the relative fitness of each candidate – as measured against his competitors – for the position sought. Scoring is not on the basis of "right" and "wrong," but on a sliding scale of values ranging from "not passable" to "outstanding." As a matter of fact, it is possible to achieve a relatively low score without a single "incorrect" answer because of evident weakness in the qualities being measured.

Occasionally, an examination may consist entirely of an oral test – either an individual or a group oral. In such cases, information is sought concerning the technical knowledges and abilities of the candidate, since there has been no written examination for this purpose. More commonly, however, an oral test is used to supplement a written examination.

Who conducts interviews?

The composition of oral boards varies among different jurisdictions. In nearly all, a representative of the personnel department serves as chairman. One of the members of the board may be a representative of the department in which the candidate would work. In some cases, "outside experts" are used, and, frequently, a businessman or some other representative of the general public is asked to serve. Labor and management or other special groups may be represented. The aim is to secure the services of experts in the appropriate field.

However the board is composed, it is a good idea (and not at all improper or unethical) to ascertain in advance of the interview who the members are and what groups they represent. When you are introduced to them, you will have some idea of their backgrounds and interests, and at least you will not stutter and stammer over their names.

What should be done before the interview?

While knowledge about the board members is useful and takes some of the surprise element out of the interview, there is other preparation which is more substantive. It *is* possible to prepare for an oral interview – in several ways:

1) Keep a copy of your application and review it carefully before the interview

This may be the only document before the oral board, and the starting point of the interview. Know what education and experience you have listed there, and the sequence and dates of all of it. Sometimes the board will ask you to review the highlights of your experience for them; you should not have to hem and haw doing it.

2) Study the class specification and the examination announcement

Usually, the oral board has one or both of these to guide them. The qualities, characteristics or knowledges required by the position sought are stated in these documents. They offer valuable clues as to the nature of the oral interview. For example, if the job involves supervisory responsibilities, the announcement will usually indicate that knowledge of modern supervisory methods and the qualifications of the candidate as a supervisor will be tested. If so, you can expect such questions, frequently in the form of a hypothetical situation which you are expected to solve. NEVER go into an oral without knowledge of the duties and responsibilities of the job you seek.

3) Think through each qualification required

Try to visualize the kind of questions you would ask if you were a board member. How well could you answer them? Try especially to appraise your own knowledge and background in each area, *measured against the job sought*, and identify any areas in which you are weak. Be critical and realistic – do not flatter yourself.

4) Do some general reading in areas in which you feel you may be weak

For example, if the job involves supervision and your past experience has NOT, some general reading in supervisory methods and practices, particularly in the field of human relations, might be useful. Do NOT study agency procedures or detailed manuals. The oral board will be testing your understanding and capacity, not your memory.

5) Get a good night's sleep and watch your general health and mental attitude

You will want a clear head at the interview. Take care of a cold or any other minor ailment, and of course, no hangovers.

What should be done on the day of the interview?

Now comes the day of the interview itself. Give yourself plenty of time to get there. Plan to arrive somewhat ahead of the scheduled time, particularly if your appointment is in the fore part of the day. If a previous candidate fails to appear, the board might be ready for you a bit early. By early afternoon an oral board is almost invariably behind schedule if there are many candidates, and you may have to wait. Take along a book or magazine to read, or your application to review, but leave any extraneous material in the waiting room when you go in for your interview. In any event, relax and compose yourself.

The matter of dress is important. The board is forming impressions about you – from your experience, your manners, your attitude, and your appearance. Give your personal appearance careful attention. Dress your best, but not your flashiest. Choose conservative, appropriate clothing, and be sure it is immaculate. This is a business interview, and your appearance should indicate that you regard it as such. Besides, being well groomed and properly dressed will help boost your confidence.

Sooner or later, someone will call your name and escort you into the interview room. *This is it.* From here on you are on your own. It is too late for any more preparation. But remember, you asked for this opportunity to prove your fitness, and you are here because your request was granted.

What happens when you go in?

The usual sequence of events will be as follows: The clerk (who is often the board stenographer) will introduce you to the chairman of the oral board, who will introduce you to the other members of the board. Acknowledge the introductions before you sit down. Do not be surprised if you find a microphone facing you or a stenotypist sitting by. Oral interviews are usually recorded in the event of an appeal or other review.

Usually the chairman of the board will open the interview by reviewing the highlights of your education and work experience from your application – primarily for the benefit of the other members of the board, as well as to get the material into the record. Do not interrupt or comment unless there is an error or significant misinterpretation; if that is the case, do not hesitate. But do not quibble about insignificant matters. Also, he will usually ask you some question about your education, experience or your present job – partly to get you to start talking and to establish the interviewing "rapport." He may start the actual questioning, or turn it over to one of the other members. Frequently, each member undertakes the questioning on a particular area, one in which he is perhaps most competent, so you can expect each member to participate in the examination. Because time is limited, you may also expect some rather abrupt switches in the direction the questioning takes, so do not be upset by it. Normally, a board member will not pursue a single line of questioning unless he discovers a particular strength or weakness.

After each member has participated, the chairman will usually ask whether any member has any further questions, then will ask you if you have anything you wish to add. Unless you are expecting this question, it may floor you. Worse, it may start you off on an extended, extemporaneous speech. The board is not usually seeking more information. The question is principally to offer you a last opportunity to present further qualifications or to indicate that you have nothing to add. So, if you feel that a significant qualification or characteristic has been overlooked, it is proper to point it out in a sentence or so. Do not compliment the board on the thoroughness of their examination – they have been sketchy, and you know it. If you wish, merely say, "No thank you, I have nothing further to add." This is a point where you can "talk yourself out" of a good impression or fail to present an important bit of information. Remember, *you close the interview yourself.*

The chairman will then say, "That is all, Mr. _____, thank you." Do not be startled; the interview is over, and quicker than you think. Thank him, gather your belongings and take your leave. Save your sigh of relief for the other side of the door.

How to put your best foot forward

Throughout this entire process, you may feel that the board individually and collectively is trying to pierce your defenses, seek out your hidden weaknesses and embarrass and confuse you. Actually, this is not true. They are obliged to make an appraisal of your qualifications for the job you are seeking, and they want to see you in your best light. Remember, they must interview all candidates and a non-cooperative candidate may become a failure in spite of their best efforts to bring out his qualifications. Here are 15 suggestions that will help you:

1) Be natural – Keep your attitude confident, not cocky

If you are not confident that you can do the job, do not expect the board to be. Do not apologize for your weaknesses, try to bring out your strong points. The board is interested in a positive, not negative, presentation. Cockiness will antagonize any board member and make him wonder if you are covering up a weakness by a false show of strength.

2) Get comfortable, but don't lounge or sprawl

Sit erectly but not stiffly. A careless posture may lead the board to conclude that you are careless in other things, or at least that you are not impressed by the importance of the occasion. Either conclusion is natural, even if incorrect. Do not fuss with your clothing, a pencil or an ashtray. Your hands may occasionally be useful to emphasize a point; do not let them become a point of distraction.

3) Do not wisecrack or make small talk

This is a serious situation, and your attitude should show that you consider it as such. Further, the time of the board is limited – they do not want to waste it, and neither should you.

4) Do not exaggerate your experience or abilities

In the first place, from information in the application or other interviews and sources, the board may know more about you than you think. Secondly, you probably will not get away with it. An experienced board is rather adept at spotting such a situation, so do not take the chance.

5) If you know a board member, do not make a point of it, yet do not hide it

Certainly you are not fooling him, and probably not the other members of the board. Do not try to take advantage of your acquaintanceship – it will probably do you little good.

6) Do not dominate the interview

Let the board do that. They will give you the clues – do not assume that you have to do all the talking. Realize that the board has a number of questions to ask you, and do not try to take up all the interview time by showing off your extensive knowledge of the answer to the first one.

7) Be attentive

You only have 20 minutes or so, and you should keep your attention at its sharpest throughout. When a member is addressing a problem or question to you, give him your undivided attention. Address your reply principally to him, but do not exclude the other board members.

8) Do not interrupt

A board member may be stating a problem for you to analyze. He will ask you a question when the time comes. Let him state the problem, and wait for the question.

9) Make sure you understand the question

Do not try to answer until you are sure what the question is. If it is not clear, restate it in your own words or ask the board member to clarify it for you. However, do not haggle about minor elements.

10) Reply promptly but not hastily

A common entry on oral board rating sheets is "candidate responded readily," or "candidate hesitated in replies." Respond as promptly and quickly as you can, but do not jump to a hasty, ill-considered answer.

11) Do not be peremptory in your answers

A brief answer is proper – but do not fire your answer back. That is a losing game from your point of view. The board member can probably ask questions much faster than you can answer them.

12) Do not try to create the answer you think the board member wants

He is interested in what kind of mind you have and how it works – not in playing games. Furthermore, he can usually spot this practice and will actually grade you down on it.

13) Do not switch sides in your reply merely to agree with a board member

Frequently, a member will take a contrary position merely to draw you out and to see if you are willing and able to defend your point of view. Do not start a debate, yet do not surrender a good position. If a position is worth taking, it is worth defending.

14) Do not be afraid to admit an error in judgment if you are shown to be wrong

The board knows that you are forced to reply without any opportunity for careful consideration. Your answer may be demonstrably wrong. If so, admit it and get on with the interview.

15) Do not dwell at length on your present job

The opening question may relate to your present assignment. Answer the question but do not go into an extended discussion. You are being examined for a *new* job, not your present one. As a matter of fact, try to phrase ALL your answers in terms of the job for which you are being examined.

Basis of Rating

Probably you will forget most of these "do's" and "don'ts" when you walk into the oral interview room. Even remembering them all will not ensure you a passing grade. Perhaps you did not have the qualifications in the first place. But remembering them will help you to put your best foot forward, without treading on the toes of the board members.

Rumor and popular opinion to the contrary notwithstanding, an oral board wants you to make the best appearance possible. They know you are under pressure – but they also want to see how you respond to it as a guide to what your reaction would be under the pressures of the job you seek. They will be influenced by the degree of poise you display, the personal traits you show and the manner in which you respond.

ABOUT THIS BOOK

This book contains tests divided into Examination Sections. Go through each test, answering every question in the margin. We have also attached a sample answer sheet at the back of the book that can be removed and used. At the end of each test look at the answer key and check your answers. On the ones you got wrong, look at the right answer choice and learn. Do not fill in the answers first. Do not memorize the questions and answers, but understand the answer and principles involved. On your test, the questions will likely be different from the samples. Questions are changed and new ones added. If you understand these past questions you should have success with any changes that arise. Tests may consist of several types of questions. We have additional books on each subject should more study be advisable or necessary for you. Finally, the more you study, the better prepared you will be. This book is intended to be the last thing you study before you walk into the examination room. Prior study of relevant texts is also recommended. NLC publishes some of these in our Fundamental Series. Knowledge and good sense are important factors in passing your exam. Good luck also helps. So now study this Passbook, absorb the material contained within and take that knowledge into the examination. Then do your best to pass that exam.

EXAMINATION SECTION

EXAMINATION SECTION
TEST 1

DIRECTIONS: Each question or incomplete statement is followed by several suggested answers or completions. Select the one that BEST answers the question or completes the statement. *PRINT THE LETTER OF THE CORRECT ANSWER IN THE SPACE AT THE RIGHT.*

1. A library is in the process of conducting an annual performance evaluation. Which of the following would be an output measure that might be used in this process?

    A. Staff expenditures
    B. User satisfaction survey results
    C. Ratio of computer workstations to daily average users
    D. Ratio of interlibrary loan lending to borrowing

2. The _____ record is a separate record attached to the bibliographic record for a serial title in which the receipt of individual issues or parts is entered on an ongoing basis.

    A. holdings
    B. check-in
    C. item
    D. periodical

3. Of the following, which research tool would be most appropriate for finding where an author uses specific words or phrases?

    A. Abstract
    B. Gazetteer
    C. Dictionary
    D. Concordance

4. In library cataloging, a separately published part of a bibliographic resource, usually representing a subject category within the whole and indicated by a topical heading or an alphanumeric heading, is a(n)

    A. class
    B. scope
    C. notch
    D. section

5. The main advantage to paying an electronic journal publisher on a per-article basis, rather than subscribing to a package or database, is that

    A. hardware, browser, and networking requirements are simpler
    B. the library pays only for what it uses
    C. costs are shifted entirely to the user
    D. costs are more predictable over time

6. The Dublin Core Metadata Initiative, an international effort to develop standard mechanisms for searching online resources, has named 15 core metadata elements to be used to direct searches. Which of the following is NOT one of these?

    A. Editor   B. Rights   C. Date   D. Format

7. "Converting" electronic records means that 7.___

    A. there is a change to the underlying bit stream, but there is no change in the representation or intellectual content of the records
    B. they are moved from a proprietary legacy system that lacks software functionality to an open system
    C. they have been transferred from old storage media to new storage media with the same format specifications and without any loss in structure, content, or context
    D. they have been exported or imported from one software environment to another without the loss of structure, content, or context even though the underlying bit stream has likely been altered

8. The 3XX fields in the MARC system contain 8.___

    A. physical descriptions
    B. main entries
    C. subject added entries
    D. titles, editions, and imprints

9. In Internet user, instead of being taken to a desired Web page, instead is taken to a page that says *Error Message 404*. What has happened? 9.___

    A. Either the server is busy, or the site has moved.
    B. Special permission is needed to access the site.
    C. The file has been moved or deleted, or the URL in incorrect.
    D. The syntax used in the URL is incorrect.

10. An anthology is compiled by 6 authors. According to the MLA format, how many of the author's names should be included in a citation? 10.___

    A. 0
    B. 1
    C. 2
    D. 6

11. Which of the following is NOT an advantage of using HTML as a format for file preservation? 11.___

    A. Extensive authoring tools
    B. Improving tools for conversion-to-HTML
    C. Good standard for delivering simple text
    D. Can be viewed in any browser

12. In the MARC record, the same digits are assigned across fields in the second and third character positions of the tag to indicate data of the same type. For example, tags reading "X10" contain information about 12.___

    A. topical terms   B. bibliographic titles
    C. uniform titles   D. corporate names

13. A librarian wants to subscribe to an e-mail newsletter that contains annotations of information technology articles and other items written by a team of librarians and library staff. She is wary, however, of having her inbox clogged with unread material that arrives too frequently for her to read it all, and would prefer to have the newsletter arrive monthly. The librarian should subscribe to   13.____

    A. *Free Pint*
    B. *Edupage*
    C. *Current Cites*
    D. *NewsScan*

14. A journal's "impact factor," a measure of its relative importance, is most often defined as the _____ in a given year.   14.____

    A. number of electronic queries coming from a library database
    B. frequency of citations to its articles
    C. number of top-rated professionals or scholars who publish in it
    D. times the full-text is displayed on a library terminal

15. _____ is the online database designed and maintained since 1995 by the Library of Congress to make legislative information accessible to the public   15.____

    A. CQ
    B. NARA
    C. THOMAS
    D. FindLaw

16. The main software protocol that manages data on the Internet is   16.____

    A. TCP/IP
    B. HTTP
    C. HTML
    D. FTP

17. Which of the following is a repeatable MARC field?   17.____

    A. 100
    B. 246
    C. 250
    D. 260

18. A user seeking articles about transportation should be directed to Wilson's _____ Index.   18.____

    A. Social Sciences
    B. Business Periodicals
    C. Applied Science and Technology
    D. General Science

19. In the library literature, materials designated with the collecting level "4" in relation to a given subject are considered

    A. "out of scope"
    B. sources of basic information
    C. comprehensive and authoritative
    D. useful for the support of research in the given subject

20. In Web addresses, the hashmark is used to

    A. create a link to another location in the same document
    B. identify a port
    C. create a link to another Web page
    D. differentiate numerical characters

21. The content of a Web site is difficult to navigate, and users tend to get confused when trying to find information. The resource assessment guideline that needs to be addressed is

    A. Documentation and Credibility
    B. Ease of Use, Navigation, and Accessibility
    C. User Interface and Design
    D. Content

22. To extend the accessibility of any material that can be displayed at a library workstation to those with extremely poor vision, _____ can be used.

    A. screen reading software
    B. screen magnifying software
    C. TTY
    D. an on-screen keyboard

23. The software application needed to read files in Portable Document Format (PDF) is known as

    A. Acrobat Reader
    B. Real Page
    C. Pagemaker
    D. techexplorer Hypermedia Browser

24. In data that is prepared in the cataloging-in-publication (CIP) format and distributed in MARC format prior to a work's publication, the element that typically appears after the notes about bibliographical references or previous editions is the

    A. Library of Congress classification number
    B. statement of responsibility
    C. ISBN
    D. Dewey Decimal classification number

25. The reason for the slow pace of initial acceptance of WORM (write once, read many) technology in library archiving is that   25.____
    A. the amount of storage available on the disks is too variable to offer predictable capacity
    B. disks are not standardized and can be read only on the type of drive used to write them
    C. the data cannot be altered once it is stored
    D. the longevity of the disk media is still unknown

KEY (CORRECT ANSWERS)

1. D	6. A	11. A	16. A	21. B
2. B	7. D	12. D	17. B	22. A
3. D	8. A	13. C	18. C	23. A
4. D	9. C	14. B	19. D	24. C
5. B	10. B	15. C	20. A	25. B

TEST 2

DIRECTIONS: Each question or incomplete statement is followed by several suggested answers or completions. Select the one that BEST answers the question or completes the statement. *PRINT THE LETTER OF THE CORRECT ANSWER IN THE SPACE AT THE RIGHT.*

1. Which of the following is NOT an aggregator service? 1.____

   A. ScienceDirect
   B. JSTOR
   C. Britannica
   D. Blackwell's Electronic Journal Navigator

2. Technical service librarians are usually concerned with any of the following, EXCEPT 2.____

   A. repairing damaged materials
   B. checking in journals
   C. cataloging books
   D. checking books out

3. Materials that are published electronically are identified by their 3.____

   A. EAD
   B. DOI
   C. XLS
   D. ISBN

4. Which of the following is an example of "mobile code" that allows a Web designer to incorporate computer programs, such as Flash pages, into Web page content? 4.____

   A. Packet
   B. Worm
   C. Warez
   D. Applet

5. The abbreviation "NOP" on a publisher's invoice usually means the requested item 5.____

   A. is on back order
   B. is not in print
   C. the requested item is not published by the vendor
   D. has not yet been published, but will be in the future

6. A well-designed online catalog or bibliographic database allows the user to employ limiting parameters to restrict the retrieval or entries including the terms included in the search statement. Which of the following is NOT a common example of these "limiters?" 6.____

   A. Spelling
   B. Publication date
   C. Full-text
   D. Locally held

7. Which of the following is LEAST likely to be a guideline followed in setting up an electronic reserves (ER) system in an academic library?

   A. Restrict access to authorized users off-site, but maintain open access on-site.
   B. Limit offsite access by course and/or instructor name.
   C. Remove or suppress access at the end of every session.
   D. Post copyright warning notices.

8. Subsystems of the Internet include
   I. the World Wide Web
   II. Newsgroups
   III. Telnet
   IV. e-mail

   A. I only
   B. I, II and III
   C. II and III
   D. I, II, III and IV

9. Binary scanning at 300 dots per inch (dpi) is usually considered adequate for

   A. halftones
   B. illustrated text
   C. typed or laser-printed archival documents
   D. published text/line art

10. The systems librarian's responsibilities typically include each of the following, EXCEPT

    A. development and maintenance of hardware and software
    B. Webmaster
    C. training staff in the use of library systems
    D. interlibrary loan processing

11. A records survey is LEAST likely to be used for the purpose of determining the _____ of archival records.

    A. quality
    B. content
    C. physical quantities
    D. provenance

12. In the searching of an electronic database, which of the following might cause a "false drop?"

    A. The omission of older information
    B. Too-frequent updating of the database
    C. A word with more than one meaning
    D. Restrictions on database use

13. A group of librarians is meeting to determine the selection of electronic journals for a library's collection. One of the MOST likely disadvantages of including the reference librarian in this group is that he may not

    A. have close contact with users
    B. be accustomed to the collaborative approach
    C. be able to relinquish his primary responsibilities for long enough periods of time
    D. have experience selecting and supporting electronic resources

14. Most Internet service providers (ISPs) are built on _____ lines.

    A. 56 Kbps
    B. ISDN
    C. T-1
    D. T-3

15. Which of the following is a term used to denote a hard copy enlargement of an image on microform?

    A. Blowback
    B. Macroform
    C. Aperture card
    D. Blowup

16. On the Web or in an online bibliography, well-designed search software is capable of
    I. searching more than one database simultaneously
    II. removing duplicate record s from results when searching multiple databases
    III. viewing search terms highlighted in results
    IV. printing, e-mailing, and downloading results in various formats

    A. I only
    B. I and III
    C. III only
    D. I, II, III and IV

17. Subject heading systems do NOT

    A. assist searchers in understanding how a specific subject fits into a larger structure of knowledge
    B. divide knowledge over 30 broad categories
    C. describe what a book or article is about
    D. allow people to search by subject area

18. In order to ensure the integrity of digital archive, the origin and chain of custody of a particular file or record most be preserved. This feature of information integrity is known as

    A. content
    B. provenance
    C. content
    D. fixity

19. The creation of a Web page could involve

    I. using a dedicated Web authoring software program
    II. converting a word-processed document to HTML
    III. converting a magazine article, with images, to PDF
    IV. use the Web authoring capability of a portal

    A. I and II
    B. I, II and IV
    C. II and III
    D. II, III and IV

20. What is the general term for an indexable concept that is assigned to add depth to subject indexing, and that is not listed in the thesaurus of indexing terms because it either represents a proper name or a concept that is not yet authorized for inclusion in the bibliographic database?

    A. assigner
    B. identifier
    C. descriptor
    D. ideogram

21. The *World of Learning* is an example of a(n)

    A. concordance
    B. encyclopedia
    C. abstract
    D. directory

22. In the United States, the professional association for academic libraries and librarians is the

    A. Association of College and Research Libraries (ACRL)
    B. Association of Specialized and Cooperative Library Agencies (ASCLA)
    C. American Library Association (ALA)
    D. National Commission on Libraries and Information Science (NCLIS)

23. The module of the library automation system that is used by the public for interacting with the system is the

    A. circulation module
    B. serials module
    C. OPAC
    D. cataloging module

24. Which of the following is a synthetic classification system?

    A. Dewey Decimal
    B. Colon classification
    C. Library of Congress classification
    D. Sears List

25. Library issues concerning the USA Patriot Act include
 I. civil liberties related to privacy and confidentiality
 II. denial of access to information
 III. fair use
 IV. copyright law

   A. I and II
   B. II only
   C. II, III and IV
   D. I, II, III and IV

KEY (CORRECT ANSWERS)

1. C	6. A	11. A	16. D	21. D
2. D	7. A	12. C	17. B	22. A
3. B	8. D	13. C	18. B	23. C
4. D	9. C	14. C	19. B	24. B
5. C	10. D	15. A	20. B	25. A

EXAMINATION SECTION
TEST 1

DIRECTIONS: Each question or incomplete statement is followed by several suggested answers or completions. Select the one that BEST answers the question or completes the statement. *PRINT THE LETTER OF THE CORRECT ANSWER IN THE SPACE AT THE RIGHT.*

1. The heart of a MARC record for a separately-cataloged electronic journal is contained in the _____ fields

    A. 0XX
    B. 3XX
    C. 5XX
    D. 7XX

    1._____

2. Which of the following is NOT an online acquisitions tool?

    A. *JSTOR*
    B. *Blackwell's Collection Manager*
    C. *Books in Print*
    D. *GOBI*

    2._____

3. The in-house approach to digital imaging and preservation typically offers each of the following advantages, EXCEPT

    A. heightened security
    B. learning by doing
    C. quality assurance
    D. predictable per-image costs

    3._____

4. The publication date of a reference book is usually found on the

    A. back cover
    B. title page
    C. page immediately before the title page
    D. page immediately following the title page

    4._____

5. In the Dublin Core Metadata Initiative, an international effort to develop standard mechanisms for searching online resources, the "type" element provides information about the

    A. topic of the content of the resource, typically expressed as keywords or classification codes
    B. rights held in and over the resource
    C. nature or genre of the content of the resource
    D. extent or scope of the resource's content

    5._____

6. _____ indexing is a method in which the subject headings or descriptors assigned to documents represent simple concepts that the user must combine at the time of searching to retrieve information on a complex subject.

    A. String
    B. Assignment
    C. Pre-coordinate
    D. Post-coordinate

    6._____

7. A library server would most likely NOT be used as

   A. a terminal for searching online resources such as periodical databases
   B. a file server hosting work processing and other office software, along with staff documents and other files
   C. the host computer for the library's automation system
   D. a connection point between the library and the Internet

8. Under copyright law, any rights that eventually revert to the copyright holder when the time period or purpose stated in the contract has elapsed or been discharged are known as _____ rights.

   A. volume
   B. serial
   C. residual
   D. subsidiary

9. Research indicates that to most library professionals, _____ is the most frequently applied criterion for evaluating the appropriateness of bibliographic references.

   A. quality
   B. topicality
   C. novelty
   D. availability

10. The best way to minimize the substrate deformation and mistracking of magnetic media is to

    A. use acetate, rather than polyester
    B. limit playback as much as possible
    C. store the media in constant temperature and humidity
    D. store the media in a room that is warmer and more humid than the rest of the library

11. Which of the following is NOT an advantage associated with purchasing an electronic journal collection in the form of a commercially packaged product?

    A. Good way to track usage
    B. Searchability of articles from other publishers
    C. Lower price per title
    D. Single search interface

12. In the Dewey Decimal Classification System, works in Natural Sciences and Mathematics are classified in the number category

    A. 000
    B. 300
    C. 500
    D. 700

13. A library's OPAC allows users to turn off images in Web pages and see only the text during searches. This is an example of interface management called   13._____

    A. ghosting
    B. graceful degradation
    C. funneling
    D. cache emptying

14. Which of the following events in library automation occurred FIRST?   14._____

    A. The growing importance of "add-ons" related to the delivery of digital content
    B. Integration into the Web environment
    C. The development of the machine-readable catalog record (MARC)
    D. Integration of library systems with learning management systems

15. One of the main advantages associated with searching for information using print indexes is that they   15._____

    A. provide cross-references to other topics
    B. are usually faster than online searches
    C. tend to yield information that is more accurate
    D. are usually more current

16. Which of the following statements about online link resolvers is FALSE?   16._____

    A. They are applications designed to match source citations with target resources.
    B. Most do not store data, but merely establish links.
    C. Most accept citation information in the form of an OpenURL.
    D. They are designed to take into account which materials a user is authorized by subscription or licensing agreement to access.

17. The intended purpose of copyright law is NOT to   17._____

    A. deter others from plagiarizing a work
    B. ensure a fair return on an author's or publisher's investment of time and money into the creation of a work
    C. provide an author or publisher with the incentive to produce a work by granting a limited monopoly
    D. reward innovators at the expense of consumers

18. When using a library's OPAC, a patron moves the mouse to pass a cursor over an image in the Web page and holds the cursor over the image for several seconds. A text message pops up, replacing the information content of the image. This feature, designed for visually impaired users, is enabled by the use of _____ in coding the page.   18._____

    A. applets
    B. alt tags
    C. plug-ins
    D. SGML

19. A search of a database containing 100 records relevant to a topic retrieves 50 records, 25 of which are relevant to the topic. The search is said to have a _____ percent recall.

    A. 10
    B. 25
    C. 50
    D. 75

19.____

20. In a bibliography compiled in the MLA format, the authorship of a book by Tom and Bridget Jones would be indicated

    A. Jones, Tom and Bridget Jones
    B. Jones, Tom and Bridget
    C. Jones, Tom and Jones, Bridget
    D. Tom Jones and Bridget Jones

20.____

21. In most large libraries, the _____ record is attached to the bibliographic record for a serial title or multivolume item to track issues, parts, or volumes as they are acquired by the library.

    A. item
    B. check-in
    C. order
    D. holdings

21.____

22. Which of the following is an online bibliographic database vendor that charges on a per-search basis?

    A. EBSCO
    B. FirstSearch
    C. ProQuest
    D. Gale Group

22.____

23. What is the term for the blending of current and emerging technologies into a single multi-use device?

    A. Virtual reality
    B. Convergence
    C. Processing
    D. Artificial intelligence

23.____

24. Which of the following is an approach to interoperability that uses proxies as interfaces between existing systems?

    A. HotJava
    B. TeX
    C. InfoBus
    D. STARTS

24.____

25. The Metadata Object Description Schema, or MODS,
    I. is an XML schema
    II. was created by the Library of Congress for representing MARC-like semantics
    III. can be used to carry selected data from MARC21 records
    IV. cannot be used for the conversion of MARC to XML without loss of data

    A. I and II
    B. I, II and IV
    C. II and III
    D. I, II, III and IV

25._____

KEY (CORRECT ANSWERS)

1.	C	11.	B
2.	A	12.	C
3.	D	13.	B
4.	D	14.	C
5.	C	15.	A
6.	D	16.	B
7.	A	17.	D
8.	C	18.	B
9.	B	19.	B
10.	C	20.	A

21. D
22. B
23. B
24. C
25. D

TEST 2

DIRECTIONS: Each question or incomplete statement is followed by several suggested answers or completions. Select the one that BEST answers the question or completes the statement. *PRINT THE LETTER OF THE CORRECT ANSWER IN THE SPACE AT THE RIGHT.*

1. The main advantage to using an intermediary service for access to electronic journals is that

    A. one search engine will search the contents of journals from several publishers and/or disciplines
    B. the one-time start-up cost is predictable
    C. the databases will have citations and abstracts only for articles that are available in full-text
    D. the depth of backfiles is predictable

    1.____

2. A library automation system needs to be able to search compatible resources from a single interface, and to search text files based on keywords.
The standard query language that is used for this is

    A. WAIS
    B. Gopher
    C. ODBC
    D. Z39.50

    2.____

3. Under copyright law, the rights to publish a work in a form other than the original publication–for example, in installments in a periodical–are known as _____ rights.

    A. residual
    B. subsidiary
    C. site-specific
    D. residual

    3.____

4. _____ indexing is a method in which multiple concepts are combined by the indexer to form subject headings or descriptors assigned to documents dealing with complex subjects.

    A. Derivative
    B. Pre-coordinate
    C. String
    D. Post-coordinate

    4.____

5. Which of the following terms is associated with efforts to bridge the digital divide?

    A. E-rate
    B. Intellectual property
    C. Artificial intelligence
    D. Convergence

    5.____

6. After deciding to offer users online access to an electronic journals collection through the library's online catalog, a library must decide whether to use the "single-record" or "separate-record" approach to offering access to print and electronic versions. Advantages of the separate-record approach include the fact that it is
   I. better suited to handle linking relationships between formats
   II. it is prescribed by AACR2 (Anglo-American Cataloging Rules)
   III. used by the Government Printing Office (GPO)
   IV. preferred by the Cooperative Online Serials Program (CONSER)

   A. I only
   B. II and III
   C. I, II and IV
   D. I, II, III and IV

7. One of the key issues in remote access to library automated systems today is

   A. authentication
   B. free speech
   C. cost
   D. training

8. Which of the following is NOT a multiple-access database?

   A. A printed dictionary arranged alphabetically by headword
   B. A library catalog searchable by author, title, subject, and keywords
   C. A bibliographic database searchable by author, title, subject, or date
   D. A printed encyclopedia in alphabetical sections, with a subject or keyword index to the entire work at the end of the last volume.

9. Which of the following services is LEAST likely to be offered by a jobber?

   A. Approval plans
   B. Continuation orders
   C. Technical processing
   D. Online searchable bibliographies

10. Modern (5th generation) computers are most specifically characterized by the feature of

    A. transistors
    B. integrated chips
    C. multiprocessing
    D. data communications

11. In library acquisitions, a purchase order becomes a contract when

    A. the seller receives the invoice
    B. it is accepted by the purchaser
    C. the purchaser signs the invoice
    D. it is accepted by the seller

12. The primary metadata that describes a social science data set is a

    A. codebook   B. unicode
    C. chapbook   D. METS

13. The contents of a single CD-ROM are roughly equivalent to the contents of about _____ books.

    A. 15
    B. 120
    C. 300
    D. 250

14. Which of the following is NOT a link resolver?

    A. ICate
    B. PURL
    C. SFX
    D. Linkfinder Plus

15. Historical works are classified in the Library of Congress Classification System under the broad category designated

    A. L
    B. H
    C. D
    D. S

16. The most widely used medium for offline data storage is

    A. CD-ROM
    B. RAID
    C. DVD-ROM
    D. magnetic tape

17. In archives, the legal term for a record or document that is no longer in the possession of its original creator or legitimate custodian is

    A. dangler
    B. estray
    C. abductee
    D. orphan

18. The largest unit in a database is a

    A. file
    B. record
    C. subfield
    D. field

19. Which of the following is NOT typically part of an item record?

    A. Price
    B. Volume number
    C. Vendor
    D. Barcode

20. Which of the following is an advantage associated with the "scan-first" approach to preservation-in which microfilm records are produced from digitized scans of original documents?   20._____

    A. Wide range of equipment and service vendors
    B. Unsettled standards for preservation
    C. Adjustments can be made prior to conversion
    D. Higher image resolution than analog photography

21. Communications from an author to the editor of a journal typically do NOT include   21._____

    A. proof of permission
    B. referee comments
    C. article appropriate query
    D. copyright assignment

22. Which of the following is NOT a primary source?   22._____

    A. Memoir/autobiography
    B. Encyclopedia
    C. Minutes from an organization or agency
    D. Speech

23. A user initiates an online search by typing "author = Shakespeare."   23._____
    This is an example of a _____ search.

    A. fielded
    B. Boolean
    C. full-text
    D. stop-list

24. Asyndetic references or bibliographies   24._____

    A. lack descriptors
    B. include embedded hypertext
    C. focus on semantic relationships between topics
    D. lack cross-references

25. The most universally accepted criteria for weeding library items are based on   25._____

    A. subject area
    B. date of publication
    C. the condition or physical description of the item
    D. content

KEY (CORRECT ANSWERS)

1.	A	11.	D
2.	D	12.	A
3.	B	13.	C
4.	B	14.	B
5.	A	15.	C
6.	C	16.	D
7.	A	17.	B
8.	A	18.	A
9.	D	19.	C
10.	C	20.	C

21. B
22. B
23. A
24. D
25. C

EXAMINATION SECTION
TEST 1

DIRECTIONS: Each question or incomplete statement is followed by several suggested answers or completions. Select the one that BEST answers the question or completes the statement. *PRINT THE LETTER OF THE CORRECT ANSWER IN THE SPACE AT THE RIGHT.*

1. A book about the life of another person is called a(n)

    A. monograph B. fiction C. biography
    D. autobiography E. reference

2. A book about real experiences is usually referred to as a(n)

    A. reference B. monograph C. fiction
    D. non-fiction E. autobiography

3. The Dewey Decimal system is a

    A. list of books, magazines, and non-print materials
    B. system for checking out books
    C. method for organizing materials
    D. system for filing cards
    E. system for networking

4. A catalog card reading MOVIE see MOTION PICTURE means:

    A. All books on movies will be found under the subject heading MOTION PICTURE
    B. Additional books on movies will be found under the subject heading MOTION PICTURE
    C. Another library has the motion picture holdings
    D. Materials are expected on motion pictures
    E. All materials on movies are circulating

5. A bibliography is a(n)

    A. encyclopedia B. networking
    C. means of circulating materials D. list of materials
    E. reference tool

6. An annotation is a(n)

    A. review B. explanatory note C. precis
    D. format E. critique

7. AMERICAN REFERENCE BOOKS ANNUAL provides a

    A. comprehensive reviewing service of reference books published in the United States
    B. monthly periodical furnishing reviews of popular reference tools
    C. publisher's guide to monthly reviewing sources
    D. professional journal published by the American Library Association
    E. bibliography of bibliographies

21

8. An index is a(n)

    A. table of contents
    B. encyclopedia
    C. series of footnotes
    D. bibliography
    E. guide to locate material

9. The library catalog is a(n)

    A. shelf list
    B. index to the materials collection
    C. bibliography
    D. system for reserves
    E. collection of book orders

10. A shelf list is a

    A. record of materials in a library
    B. reserve list
    C. weeding list
    D. list of reference materials
    E. bibliography of reference sources

11. Technical services include

    A. acquisitions, cataloging, and materials preparation
    B. reference work and user services
    C. reader's advisory services
    D. circulation and reference services
    E. networking

12. A collection of materials such as pamphlets, clippings, or illustrations kept in special containers is referred to as a

    A. card catalog
    B. card file
    C. vertical file
    D. container collection
    E. clipping file

13. An electromagnetic recording made for playback on a television set is referred to as a(n)

    A. audio tape
    B. cassette
    C. video-recording
    D. superdisk
    E. fiche

14. A word, name, object, group of words, or acronym describing a subject is usually referred to as a

    A. cross reference
    B. subject heading
    C. nom de plume
    D. serial
    E. catalog card

15. A collection of materials with restricted circulation usually found in college and university libraries is called a(n) _____ collection.

    A. reserved materials
    B. patron
    C. student
    D. open stack
    E. rotating reserve

16. An independent publication of forty-nine pages or less, bound in paper covers, is called a

    A. serial
    B. monograph
    C. microcard
    D. pamphlet
    E. fiche

17. Library work directly concerned with assistance to readers in securing information and in using library resources is termed   17.____

    A. circulation services
    B. technical services
    C. reader's advisory services
    D. user services
    E. networking

18. A three-dimensional representation of a real object reproduced in the original size or to scale is called a(n)   18.____

    A. model
    B. film
    C. microform
    D. ultrafiche
    E. videotape

19. The act of filling out required forms to become an eligible library borrower is called   19.____

    A. serialization
    B. direction
    C. registration
    D. reference work
    E. signing

20. A direction in a catalog that guides the user to related names or subjects is termed a _____ reference.   20.____

    A. shelf
    B. see-also
    C. title
    D. see
    E. subject

21. A record of a work in the catalog under the title is called a   21.____

    A. subject card
    B. number entry
    C. author card
    D. subject entry
    E. title entry

22. The printed scheme of a classification system is referred to as a   22.____

    A. classification schedule
    B. numbering schedule
    C. lettering schedule
    D. cutter number
    E. copyright

23. The entry of a work in the catalog under the subject heading is called a   23.____

    A. subject card
    B. subject heading
    C. subject entry
    D. reference entry
    E. subject guide

24. The department in a library responsible for officially listing prospective borrowers is the _____ department.   24.____

    A. reference
    B. registration
    C. welcoming
    D. circulation
    E. technical

25. Library work that deals with patrons and the use of the library collection is called _____ services.   25.____

    A. technical
    B. reader
    C. circulation
    D. reference
    E. public

KEY (CORRECT ANSWERS)

1. C
2. D
3. C
4. A
5. D

6. B
7. A
8. E
9. B
10. A

11. A
12. C
13. C
14. B
15. A

16. D
17. D
18. A
19. C
20. B

21. E
22. A
23. C
24. B
25. D

TEST 2

DIRECTIONS: Each question or incomplete statement is followed by several suggested answers or completions. Select the one that BEST answers the question or completes the statement. *PRINT THE LETTER OF THE CORRECT ANSWER IN THE SPACE AT THE RIGHT.*

1. Material held for a borrower for a limited time is termed _____ material.   1._____
    - A. reference
    - B. reserved
    - C. circulation
    - D. special
    - E. held

2. A notice sent to a borrower to remind him to return heldover due material is a(n)   2._____
    - A. warning
    - B. notice
    - C. overdue notice
    - D. warning notice
    - E. call slip

3. Material returned to the library before the date due is   3._____
    - A. Penalized
    - B. returned
    - C. accepted
    - D. unneeded
    - E. subject to examination

4. Real objects, specimens, or artifacts are called   4._____
    - A. toys
    - B. realia
    - C. games
    - D. opaque material
    - E. models

5. A film with a series of pictures in sequence which creates the illusion of motion when projected is classified as a   5._____
    - A. photogram
    - B. motion picture
    - C. videotape
    - D. cassette
    - E. slide

6. Laying books on the shelves in proper order is called   6._____
    - A. placing
    - B. weeding
    - C. reading
    - D. shifting
    - E. shelving

7. A publication issued in successive parts usually to be continued indefinitely is referred to as a   7._____
    - A. paper
    - B. monograph
    - C. serial
    - D. pamphlet
    - E. edition

8. A record of the loan of material is called a   8._____
    - A. call slip
    - B. reserve
    - C. contract
    - D. copy
    - E. charge

9. Information arranged in tabular, outline, or graphic form on a sheet of paper is called a   9._____
    - A. classification
    - B. charge
    - C. chart
    - D. catalog
    - E. cartoon

10. The method used to lend materials to borrowers and maintain the necessary records is the _____ system.   10._____
    - A. classification
    - B. circulation control
    - C. reference
    - D. borrowing
    - E. returnable

25

11. Any entry, other than a subject entry, that is made in a catalog in addition to the main entry is called a(n)

    A. added entry B. call number C. central reference
    D. reference entry E. explanatory entry

12. The record of the number of items charged out of a library is termed

    A. record statistics B. circulation statistics
    C. circulation control D. record control
    E. itemizing

13. A number assigned to each book or item as it is received by the library is referred to as a(n) _____ number.

    A. call B. accession C. entry
    D. acquisition E. ordering

14. A master file of all registered borrowers in a library system is called the _____ file.

    A. personnel B. charging C. classification
    D. central registration E. circulation control

15. A person who charges out materials from a library is called the

    A. lender B. technician C. professional librarian
    D. clerk E. borrower

16. A catalog in which all entries are filed in alphabetical order is called a(n) _____ catalog.

    A. card B. Library of Congress C. alphabetical
    D. dictionary E. subject

17. The day material is to be returned to a library is usually referred to as the _____ day.

    A. library B. date-due C. return
    D. book E. library-due

18. The act of annulling the library's record of a loan is called

    A. discharging B. cancelling C. stamping
    D. recording E. unloaning

19. The penalty charge for material returned after the date due is called a(n)

    A. charge B. fine C. tax D. levy E. arrangement

20. A set of materials containing rules designed to be played in a competitive situation is called a

    A. rolodome B. game C. sketch D. linedex E. materialsset

21. A catalog in more than one part is termed a _____ catalog.

    A. divided B. split C. Library of Congress
    D. Dewey E. Sears

22. A metal file containing a number of flat metal leaves that hold single cardboard strips listing titles and holdings is called a   22._____

    A. linedesk B. linetop C. rolotop
    D. rotofile E. linedex

23. A metal file containing a number of shallow drawers in which serial check-in cards are kept is usually referred to as a   23._____

    A. linedesk B. rotofile C. box D. kardex E. linetop

24. The strip of paper pasted in the book or on the book packet, on which the date due is stamped, is called the   24._____

    A. date slip B. date card C. date strip
    D. call slip E. card strip

25. Film on which materials have been photographed in greatly reduced size is called   25._____

    A. minifilm B. microfilm C. photogram
    D. miniaturization E. photoreduction

KEY (CORRECT ANSWERS)

1.	B	11.	A
2.	C	12.	B
3.	C	13.	B
4.	B	14.	D
5.	B	15.	E
6.	E	16.	D
7.	C	17.	B
8.	E	18.	A
9.	C	19.	B
10.	B	20.	B

21. A
22. E
23. D
24. A
25. B

EXAMINATION SECTION
TEST 1

DIRECTIONS: Each question or incomplete statement is followed by several suggested answers or completions. Select the one that BEST answers the question or completes the statement. *PRINT THE LETTER OF THE CORRECT ANSWER IN THE SPACE AT THE RIGHT.*

1. An employee requests a book which is not in the department library.
   Of the following, the MOST advisable course of action for you to take is to

   A. attempt to get the book for him by means of the department's affiliation with the public library
   B. explain that the book is not available from the department's library
   C. suggest that he try his local public library and give him a list of local libraries
   D. tell him where he may purchase the book and offer to make the purchase for him

   1.____

2. The catalog for the use of department employees has just been thoroughly checked and revised by a professional librarian. After trying to find the name of a book in the catalog, an employee tells you that he cannot find it.
   Of the following, the MOST advisable action for you to take FIRST is to

   A. call the public library for the exact title
   B. look it up in the catalog yourself
   C. look through the stacks for the book
   D. tell him you are sorry but the book is not in the department library

   2.____

3. You find that three pages are missing from one of the copies of a very popular book in the department library.
   Of the following, the MOST advisable action for you to take is to

   A. discard the book since its usefulness is now sharply curtailed
   B. order another copy of the book but keep the old copy until the new one is received
   C. report the fact to the head of the department and request further instructions
   D. type copies of the pages from another volume of the book and tape them in the appropriate place

   3.____

4. The department library is scheduled to close at 5 P.M. It is now 4:55, and an employee reading a book shows no signs of leaving.
   Of the following, the MOST advisable action for you to take is to

   A. tell him it is time to leave
   B. tell him the time and ask him if he wishes to borrow the book
   C. turn the lights off and on, indirectly suggesting that he leave
   D. wait until he decides to leave

   4.____

5. The dealer from whom you have been buying books for the department library has informed you that henceforth he can give you only a fifteen percent instead of a twenty percent discount.
   Of the following, the MOST advisable course of action for you to take FIRST is to

   5.____

A. accept the fifteen percent discount
B. inform the head of your department
C. investigate the discount given by other book dealers
D. order directly from the publishers

6. Your supervisor is a professional librarian and is responsible for the selection of material to be added to the department library in which you are an employee. Shortly after you start on the job, an employee of the department brings you a written request to have several books of his choice added to the library.
Of the following, the MOST advisable course of action for you to take is to

   A. order the books immediately
   B. pass the suggestion along to your supervisor
   C. refuse to accept his suggestion
   D. tell him that he will have to buy the books

7. You object to your supervisor's plan to change the system in the department library from closed to open stacks.
Of the following, the MOST advisable course of action for you to take is to

   A. ask other members of the staff to support your objections
   B. await further instructions and then do as you are told
   C. discuss your objections with your supervisor
   D. send a brief report of your objections to the department head

8. Two weeks after you begin working in the department library, you learn that books in library bindings last twice as long as those with the publishers' bindings.
Of the following, the MOST advisable course of action for you to follow is to

   A. buy only paperbound books
   B. have all new books put in library bindings
   C. put in library bindings only rare editions
   D. put in library bindings only those books likely to get hard use

9. Your superior is away on an official trip. You have been asked to type and e-mail several hundred letters before he returns. Just as you begin the job, the computer breaks down.
Of the following, the MOST advisable course of action for you to take is to

   A. arrange to have the computer serviced as soon as possible
   B. write the letters by hand
   C. postpone the job until after your supervisor returns
   D. write to your supervisor for advice

10. Your supervisor in the department library is out for the day. You receive a telephone call from another city department asking if they may borrow one of the books in your library.
Of the following, the MOST advisable action for you to take FIRST is to tell the department

    A. that books are not permitted out of the department
    B. that you will check and call back the next day
    C. to send a representative to inquire the next day
    D. to write a letter to the department head

11. Two months have passed since the head of the department has borrowed one of the books in the department library. Of the following, the MOST advisable action for you to take is to

    A. ask the department head if he wishes to keep the book out longer
    B. leave a note for the department head telling him that the book should be returned immediately
    C. wait another month and then write the book off as lost
    D. wait until you receive another request for the book

11.____

12. Your supervisor tells you that he would like to have all old book cards replaced, all torn pages mended, and the books put in good condition in all other respects by the following day. You know that this is an impossible task.
    Of the following, the MOST advisable course of action for you to take is to

    A. attempt to finish as much of the job as possible
    B. explain the difficulties involved to the supervisor and await further instruction
    C. ignore the request since it is completely unreasonable
    D. make a complaint to the head of the department

12.____

13. The library in which you work has received about fifty new books. These books must be cataloged, but you have had no experience in this type of work. However, you have been told that a professional librarian will join the staff in about six weeks.
    Of the following, the MOST advisable course of action for you to take in the meantime is to

    A. close the library for a week and try to do the cataloging yourself
    B. lend the books only to those who can get special permission
    C. let the users take the books even though they are not cataloged
    D. put all the books in storage until they can be cataloged

13.____

14. The hospital library in which you work has a large back-log of books that need to be mended. You are unable to do more than a small part of the job by yourself. One of the patients in the hospital has done book binding and mending. He offers to help you because he sees the need for doing the job and because he wants something to do with his hands.
    Of the following, the MOST advisable course of action for you to take is to

    A. accept his offer on condition that the doctor approves
    B. ask him to push the book cart around the wards so you will be free to do the mending
    C. refuse his offer
    D. write a letter to his former employer to find out whether he is a good bookbinder

14.____

15. You accidentally spill a glass of water over an open book.
    Of the following, the MOST advisable action for you to take FIRST in most cases is to

    A. discard the book to prevent the water from spoiling other material
    B. hang the book up by its binding
    C. press the covers together to squeeze out the water
    D. separate the wet pages with blotters

15.____

16. In mending a book, you overturn a jar of glue on a new book.
Of the following, the MOST advisable action for you to take FIRST is to

    A. allow the glue to harden so that it may be peeled off
    B. attempt to wipe off the glue with any clean scrap paper
    C. discard the book to prevent other materials from being spoiled
    D. report the incident immediately to your supervisor

17. Of the following, the situation LEAST likely to result in injury to books is one in which

    A. all books support each other standing upright
    B. short books are placed between tall ones
    C. the books are as close together as possible
    D. the books lean against the sides of the shelves

18. Of the following, a damp cloth may BEST be used to clean a cloth book cover that has been coated with

    A. benzene   B. gold leaf
    C. turpentine   D. varnish

19. Decay of leather bindings may be MOST effectively delayed by

    A. a short tanning period
    B. air conditioning
    C. rubbing periodically with a damp cloth
    D. treatment with heat

20. When paste is used to mend a page, it is MOST desirable that the page should then be

    A. aired   B. heated   C. pressed   D. sprayed

21. A book that is perfectly clean but has been used by someone with chicken pox can probably BEST be handled by

    A. burning, followed by proper disposal of the ashes
    B. forty-eight hour exposure to ultraviolet light
    C. keeping it out of circulation for six months
    D. treating it the same as any other book

22. The BEST combination of temperature and humidity for books is temperature _____ degrees, humidity _____.

    A. 50-60; 20-30%   B. 60-70; 10-20%
    C. 60-70; 50-60%   D. 70-80; 70-80%

23. When a new book is received, it is LEAST important to keep a record of the

    A. author's name
    B. cost of the book
    C. number of pages
    D. source from which it was obtained

24. You have just received from the publisher a new book for the department library, but you find that the binding is torn.
    Of the following, the MOST advisable action for you to take is to

    A. mend the binding and take no further action
    B. mend the binding but claim a price discount
    C. report the damage to the department head
    D. send the book back to the publisher

25. Of the following, a characteristic of MOST photographic charging systems is that

    A. book cards are not used
    B. charging is done by one person
    C. date due is stamped on borrower's card
    D. transaction cards are not used

KEY (CORRECT ANSWERS)

1. A
2. B
3. D
4. B
5. C

6. B
7. C
8. D
9. A
10. B

11. A
12. B
13. C
14. A
15. D

16. B
17. A
18. D
19. B
20. C

21. D
22. C
23. C
24. D
25. B

TEST 2

DIRECTIONS: Each question or incomplete statement is followed by several suggested answers or completions. Select the one that BEST answers the question or completes the statement. *PRINT THE LETTER OF THE CORRECT ANSWER IN THE SPACE AT THE RIGHT.*

1. In a card catalog, a reference from one subject heading to another is MOST commonly called a(n) _____ reference.   1.____

   A. cross   B. direct   C. primary   D. indirect

2. A book which is shortened by omission of detail but which retains the general sense of the original is called a(n)   2.____

   A. compendium   B. manuscript
   C. miniature   D. abridgment

3. An anonymous book is a   3.____

   A. book published before 1500
   B. book whose author is unknown
   C. copy which is defective
   D. work that is out of print

4. All the letters, figures, and symbols assigned to a book to indicate its location on library shelves comprise the _____ number.   4.____

   A. call   B. Cutter   C. index   D. inventory

5. The term *format* does NOT refer to a book's   5.____

   A. binding   B. size
   C. theme   D. typography

6. The term *card catalog* USUALLY refers to a   6.____

   A. catalog consisting of loose-leaf pages upon which the cards are pasted
   B. catalog in which entries are on separate cards arranged in a definite order
   C. catalog of the cards available from the Library of Congress
   D. record on cards of the works which have been weeded out of the library collection

7. The term *circulation record* USUALLY refers to a record of   7.____

   A. daily attendance
   B. the books borrowed
   C. the most popular books
   D. the books out on interlibrary loan

8. Reading shelves USUALLY involves checking the shelves to see that all the books   8.____

   A. are in the correct order
   B. are suitable for the library's patrons
   C. are there
   D. have been cataloged correctly

9. In an alphabetical catalog of book titles and authors' names, the name *de Santis* would be filed

    A. after *DeWitt*
    B. after *Sanders*
    C. before AND THEN THERE WERE NONE
    D. before *Deutsch*

10. In typing, the Shift key on the computer keyboard is used to

    A. change the font size
    B. indent a line of text
    C. type numbers
    D. type capitals

11. The abbreviation e.g. means *most nearly*

    A. as follows
    B. for example
    C. refer to
    D. that is

12. The abbreviation ff. means *most nearly*

    A. and following pages
    B. formerly
    C. frontispiece
    D. the end

13. The abbreviation ibid. means *most nearly*

    A. consult the index
    B. in the same place
    C. see below
    D. turn the page

14. *Ex libris* is a Latin phrase meaning

    A. former librarian
    B. from the books
    C. without charge
    D. without liberty

15. An expurgated edition of a book is one which

    A. contains many printing errors
    B. includes undesirable passages
    C. is not permitted in public libraries
    D. omits objectionable material

16. The re-charging of a book to a borrower is USUALLY called

    A. fining
    B. processing
    C. reissue
    D. renewal

17. A sheet of paper that is pierced with holes is

    A. borated
    B. collated
    C. perforated
    D. serrated

18. *Glossary* means *most nearly* a(n)

    A. dictionary of selected terms in a particular book or field
    B. list of chapter headings in the order in which they appear in a book
    C. section of the repairing division which coats books with a protective lacquer
    D. alphabetical table of the contents of a book

19. *Accessioning* means *most nearly* 19.____

    A. acquiring books
    B. arranging books for easy access
    C. donating books as gifts
    D. listing books in the order of purchase

20. *Bookplate* means *most nearly* 20.____

    A. a label in a book showing who owns it
    B. a metal device for holding books upright
    C. a rounded zinc surface upon which a page is printed
    D. the flat part of the binding of a book

21. *Thesaurus* means *most nearly* a book which 21.____

    A. contains instructions on how to prepare a thesis
    B. contains words grouped according to similarity of meaning
    C. describes the techniques of dramatic acting
    D. gives quotations from well-known works of literature

22. *Salacious* means *most nearly* 22.____

    A. careful   B. delicious   C. lewd   D. salty

23. *Pseudonym* means *most nearly* 23.____

    A. false report   B. fictitious name
    C. libelous statement   D. psychic phenomenon

24. *Gamut* means *most nearly* a(n) 24.____

    A. bookworm   B. simpleton
    C. vagrant   D. entire range

25. *Monograph* means *most nearly* a 25.____

    A. machine for duplicating typewritten material by means of a stencil
    B. picture reproduced on an entire page of a manuscript
    C. single chart used to represent statistical data
    D. systematic treatise on a particular subject

KEY (CORRECT ANSWERS)

1. A
2. D
3. B
4. A
5. C

6. B
7. B
8. A
9. D
10. D

11. B
12. A
13. B
14. B
15. D

16. D
17. C
18. A
19. D
20. A

21. B
22. C
23. B
24. D
25. D

TEST 3

DIRECTIONS: Each question or incomplete statement is followed by several suggested answers or completions. Select the one that BEST answers the question or completes the statement. *PRINT THE LETTER OF THE CORRECT ANSWER IN THE SPACE AT THE RIGHT.*

Questions 1-15.

DIRECTIONS: Questions 1 through 15 are to be answered SOLELY on the basis of the information contained in the following passage.

Machines may be useful for bibliographic purposes, but they will be useful only if we study the bibliographic requirements to be met and the machines available, in terms of each job which needs to be done. Many standard tools now available are more efficient than high-speed machines if the machines are used as gadgets rather than as the mechanical elements of well-considered systems.

It does not appear impossible for us to learn to think in terms of scientific management to such an extent that we may eventually be able to do much of the routine part of bibliographic work mechanically with greater efficiency, both in terms of cost per unit of service and in terms of management of the intellectual content of literature. There are many bibliographic tasks which will probably not be done mechanically in the near future because the present tools appear to present great advantages over any machine in sight; for example, author bibliography done on the electronic machines would appear to require almost as much work in instructing the machine as is required to look in an author catalog. The major field of usefulness of the machines would appear to be that of subject bibliography, and particularly in research rather than quick reference jobs.

Machines now available or in sight cannot answer a quick reference question either as fast or as economically as will consultation of standard reference works such as dictionaries, encyclopedias, or almanacs, nor would it appear worthwhile to instruct a machine and run the machine to pick out one recent book or "any recent book" in a broad subject field. It would appear, therefore, that high-speed electronic or electrical machinery may be used for bibliographic purposes only in research institutions, at least for the next five or ten years, and their use will probably be limited to research problems in those institutions. It seems quite probable that during the next decade electronic machines, including the Rapid Selector, which was designed with bibliographic purposes in mind, will find application in administrative, office, and business uses to a much greater extent than they will in bibliographic operations.

The shortcomings of machines used as gadgets have been stressed in this paper. Nevertheless, the use of machines for bibliographic purposes is developing, and it is developing rapidly. It appears quite certain that several of the machines and mechanical devices can now perform certain of the routine operations involved in bibliographic work more accurately and more efficiently than these operations can be performed without them.

At least one machine, the Rapid Selector, appears potentially capable of performing higher orders of bibliographic work than we have been able to perform in the past, if and when we learn: (a) what is really needed for the advancement of learning in the way of bibliographic services; and (b) how to utilize the machine efficiently.

There is no magic in machines as such. There will be time-lag in their application, just as there was with the typewriter. The speed and efficiency in handling the mechanical part of bibliographic work, which will determine the point of diminishing returns, depend in large measure on how long it will be before we approach these problems from the point of view of scientific management.

This report cannot solve the problem of bibliographic organization. Machines alone cannot solve the problem. We need to develop systems of handling the mass of bibliographic material, but such systems cannot be developed until we discover and establish our objectives, our plans, our standards, our methods and controls, within the framework of each situation. This may take twenty years or it may take one hundred, but it will come. The termination of how long the time-lag will be rests upon our time-lag in gathering objective information upon which scientific management of literature can be based.

1. On the basis of the above passage, machines will *probably* be MOST useful in

    A. determining the cost per unit of service
    B. quick reference jobs
    C. subject bibliography
    D. title cataloging

2. On the basis of the above passage, the Rapid Selector will *probably* be LEAST used during the next ten years in

    A. administration   B. bibliographic work
    C. business   D. office work

3. It may be inferred from the above passage that is is NOT practical to use machines to do author bibliography because

    A. experienced machine operators are not available
    B. more than one machine is needed for such a task
    C. the results obtained from a machine are unreliable
    D. too much work is involved in instructing the machine

4. On the basis of the above passage, one of the criteria of efficiency is the

    A. amount of work required   B. cost per unit of service
    C. net cost of service   D. number of machines available

5. On the basis of the above passage, the LEAST efficient of the following for quick reference jobs are

    A. bibliographies   B. dictionaries
    C. encyclopedias   D. machines

6. On the basis of the above passage, in the next few years, high-speed electronic machinery will probably be used for bibliographic purposes only by

    A. civil engineers
    B. institutions of higher education
    C. publishers
    D. research institutions

7. On the basis of the above passage, the Rapid Selector was designed for use in handling   7.____

   A. bibliographic operations
   B. computing problems
   C. photographic reproduction
   D. standard reference works

8. On the basis of the above passage, progress on the development of machines to do bibliographic tasks has reached the point at which   8.____

   A. all present tools have become obsolete
   B. certain jobs are better performed with machines than without them
   C. machines are as efficient in doing quick reference jobs as in doing special research jobs
   D. machines are no longer regarded as being too expensive

9. The one of the following which is NOT stated by the above passage to be essential in developing ways of handling bibliographic material is   9.____

   A. discovering methods and controls
   B. establishing objectives
   C. establishing standards
   D. obtaining historical data

10. The above passage indicates that machines alone will NOT be able to solve the problem of   10.____

    A. bibliographic organization
    B. reference work
    C. scientific management
    D. system analysis

11. On the basis of the above passage, the viewpoint of scientific management is essential in   11.____

    A. developing the mechanical handling of bibliographic work
    B. operating the Rapid Selector
    C. repairing electronic machines
    D. showing that people are always superior to machines in bibliographic work

12. On the basis of the above passage, there are machines in existence which   12.____

    A. are particularly useful for statistical analysis in library work
    B. are the result of scientific management of bibliographic work
    C. have not been efficiently utilized for bibliographic work
    D. may be installed in a medium-sized library

13. On the basis of the above passage, the scientific management of literature awaits the   13.____

    A. assembling of objective information
    B. compilation of new reference books
    C. development of more complex machines
    D. development of simplified machinery

14. Based on the above passage, it may be INFERRED that the author's attitude toward the use of machines in bibliographic work is that they

   A. have limited usefulness at the present time
   B. will become useful only if scientific management is applied
   C. will probably always be restricted to routine operations
   D. will probably never be useful

15. The author of the above passage believes that high-speed machines are BEST adapted to bibliographic work when they are used

   A. as gadgets
   B. in place of standard reference works
   C. to perform complex operations
   D. to perform routine operations

Questions 16-25.

DIRECTIONS: Questions 16 through 25 deal with the classification of non-fiction books according to the Dewey Classification as outlined below. For each book listed, print in the space on the right the letter in front of the class to which it belongs.

Classification

16. Ernst. WORDS: ENGLISH ROOTS AND HOW THEY GROW
17. Faulkner. FROM VERSAILLES TO THE NEW DEAL
18. Fry. CHINESE ART
19. Kant. CRITIQUE OF PURE REASON
20. Millikan. THE ELECTRON
21. Morgan. THEORY OF THE GENE
22. Raine. THE YEAR ONE; POEMS
23. Richards. PRINCIPLES OF LITERARY CRITICISM
24. Steinberg. BASIC JUDAISM
25. Strachey. QUEEN VICTORIA

A. 000 General Works
B. 100 Philosophy
C. 200 Religion
D. 300 Social Science
E. 400 Philology
F. 500 Pure Science
G. 600 Applied Science, Useful Arts
H. 700 Fine Arts
I. 800 Literature, Belleslettres
J. 900 History, Biography

KEY (CORRECT ANSWERS)

1. C
2. B
3. D
4. B
5. D

6. D
7. A
8. B
9. D
10. A

11. A
12. C
13. A
14. A
15. D

16. E
17. J
18. H
19. B
20. F

21. F
22. I
23. I
24. C
25. J

EXAMINATION SECTION
TEST 1

DIRECTIONS: Each question or incomplete statement is followed by several suggested answers or completions. Select the one that BEST answers the question or completes the statement. *PRINT THE LETTER OF THE CORRECT ANSWER IN THE SPACE AT THE RIGHT.*

1. Good procedure in handling complaints from the public may be divided into the following four principal stages:
   I. Investigation of the complaint
   II. Receipt of the complaint
   III. Assignment of responsibility for investigation and correction
   IV. Notification of correction

   The ORDER in which these stages ordinarily come is:
   A. III, II, I, IV   B. II, III, I, IV   C. II, III, IV, I   D. II, IV, III, I

2. The department may expect the MOST severe public criticism if
   A. it asks for an increase in its annual budget
   B. it purchases new and costly street cleaning equipment
   C. sanitation officers and men are reclassified to higher salary grades
   D. there is delay in cleaning streets of snow

3. The MOST important function of public relations in the department should be to
   A. develop cooperation on the part of the public in keeping streets clean
   B. get stricter penalties enacted for health code violations
   C. recruit candidates for entrance positions who ca be developed into supervisors
   D. train career personnel so that they can advance in the department

4. The one of the following which has MOST frequently elicited unfavorable public comment has been
   A. dirty sidewalks or streets   B. dumping on lot
   C. failure to curb dogs   D. overflowing garbage cans

5. It has been suggested that, as a public relations measure, sections hold *open house* for the public.
   The MOST effective time for this would be
   A. during the summer when children are not in school and can accompany their parents
   B. during the winter when show is likely to fall and the public can see snow removal preparations
   C. immediately after a heavy snow storm when department snow removal operations are in full progress
   D. when street sanitation is receiving general attention as during *Keep City Clean* week

6. When a public agency conducts a public relations program, it is MOST likely to find that each recipient of its message will
   A. disagree with the basic purpose of the message if the officials are not well known to him
   B. accept the message if it is presented by someone perceived as having a definite intention to persuade
   C. ignore the message unless it is presented in a literate and clever manner
   D. give greater attention to certain portions of the message as a result of his individual and cultural differences

7. Following are three statements about public relations and communications:
   I. A person who seeks to influence public opinion can speed up a trend
   II. Mass communications is the exposure of a mass audience to an idea
   III. All media are equally effective in reaching opinion leaders
   Which of the following choices CORRECTLY classifies the above statements into those which are correct and those which are not?
   A. I and II are correct, but III is not.
   B. II and III are correct, but I is not.
   C. I and III are correct, but II is not.
   D. III is correct, but I and II are not.

8. Public relations experts say that MAXIMUM effect for a message results from
   A. concentrating in one medium
   B. ignoring mass media and concentrating on *opinion makers*
   C. presenting only those factors which support a given position
   D. using a combination of two or more of the available media

9. To assure credibility and avoid hostility, the public relations man MUST
   A. make certain his message is truthful, not evasive or exaggerated
   B. make sure his message contains some dire consequence if ignored
   C. repeat the message often enough so that it cannot be ignored
   D. try to reach as many people and groups as possible

10. The public relations man MUST be prepared to assume that members of his audience
    A. may have developed attitudes toward his proposals—favorable, neutral, or unfavorable
    B. will be immediately hostile
    C. will consider his proposals with an open mind
    D. will invariably need an introduction to his subject

11. The one of the following statements that is CORRECT is:
    A. When a stupid question is asked of you by the public, it should be disregarded
    B. If you insist on formality between you and the public, the public will not be able to ask stupid questions that cannot be answered
    C. The public should be treated courteously, regardless of how stupid their questions may be
    D. You should explain to the public how stupid their questions are

12. With regard to public relations, the MOST important item which should be emphasized in an employee training program is that 12.____
    A. each inspector is a public relations agent
    B. an inspector should give the public all the information it asks for
    C. it is better to make mistakes and give erroneous information than to tell the public that you do not know the correct answer to their problem
    D. public relations is so specialized a field that only persons specially trained in it should consider it

13. Members of the public frequently ask about departmental procedures. 13.____
    Of the following, it is BEST to
    A. advise the public to put the question in writing so that he can get a proper formal reply
    B. refuse to answer because this is a confidential matter
    C. explain the procedure as briefly as possible
    D. attempt to avoid the issue by discussing other matters

14. The effectiveness of a public relations program in a public agency such as the authority is BEST indicated by the 14.____
    A. amount of mass media publicity favorable to the policies of the authority
    B. morale of those employees who directly serve the patrons of the authority
    C. public's understanding and support of the authority's program and policies
    D. number of complaint received by the authority from patrons using its facilities

15. In an attempt to improve public opinion about a certain idea, the BEST course of action for an agency to take would be to present the 15.____
    A. clearest statements of the idea even though the language is somewhat technical
    B. idea as the result of long-term studies
    C. idea in association with something familiar to most people
    D. idea as the viewpoint of the majority leaders

16. The fundamental factor in any agency's community relations program is 16.____
    A. an outline of the objectives
    B. relations with the media
    C. the everyday actions of the employees
    D. a well-planned supervisory program

17. The FUNDAMENTAL factor in the success of a community relations program is 17.____
    A. true commitment by the community
    B. true commitment by the administration
    C. a well-planned, systematic approach
    D. the actions of individuals in their contacts with the public

18. The statement below which is LEAST correct is:
    A. Because of selection standards, the supervisor frequently encounters problems resulting from subordinates' inability to express themselves in the language of the profession.
    B. Distortion of the meaning of a communication is usually brought about by a failure to use language that has a precise meaning to others.
    C. The term *filtering* is the distortion or dilution of content of a communication that occurs as information is passed from individual to individual.
    D. The complexity of the *communications net* will directly affect.

19. Consider the following three statements that may or may not be CORRECT:
    I. In order to prevent the stifling of communications flow, supervisors should insist that employees use the formal communications network.
    II. Two-way communications are faster and more accurate than one-way communications.
    III. There is a direct correlation between the effectiveness of communications and the total setting in which they occur.
    The choice below which MOST accurately describes the above statement is:
    A. All three are correct.
    B. All three are incorrect.
    C. More than one statement is correct.
    D. Only one of the statements is correct.

20. The statement below which is MOST inaccurate is:
    A. The supervisor's most important tool in learning whether or not he is communicating well is feedback.
    B. Follow-up is essential if useful feedback is to be obtained.
    C. Subordinates are entitled, as a matter of right, to explanations from management concerning the reasons for orders or directives.
    D. A skilled supervisor is often able to use the grapevine to good advantage.

21. *Since concurrence by those affected is not sought, this kind of communication can be issued with relative ease.*
    The kind of communication being referred to in this quotation is
    A. autocratic   B. democratic   C. directive   D. free-rein

22. The statement below which is LEAST correct is:
    A. Clarity is more important in oral communicating than in written since the readers of a written communication can read it over again.
    B. Excessive use of abbreviations in written communications should be avoided.
    C. Short sentences with simple words are preferred over complex sentences and difficult words in a written communication.
    D. The *newspaper* style of writing ordinarily simplifies expression and facilitates understanding.

23. Which one of the following is the MOST important factor for the department to consider in building a good public image?
    A. A good working relationship with the news media
    B. An efficient community relations program
    C. An efficient system for handling citizen complaints
    D. The proper maintenance of facilities and equipment
    E. The behavior of individuals in their contacts with the public.

24. It has been said that the ability to communicate clearly and concisely is the MOST important single skill of the supervisor.
    Consider the following statements:
    I. The adage, *Actions speak louder than words*, has NO application in superior/subordinate communications since good communications are accomplished with words.
    II. The environment in which a communication takes place will *rarely* determine its effect.
    III. Words are symbolic representations which must be associated with past experience or else they are meaningless.
    The choice below which MOST accurately describes the above statements is:
    A. I, II, and III are correct.
    B. I and II are correct, but III is not.
    C. I and III are correct, but II is not.
    D. III is correct, but I and II are not.
    E. I, II, and III are incorrect.

25. According to expert opinion, the effectiveness of an organization is very dependent upon good upward, downward, and lateral communications. Lateral communications are most important to the activity of coordinating the efforts of organizational units. Before real communication can take place at any level, barriers to communication must be recognized, understood, and removed.
    Consider the following three statements:
    I. The *principal* barrier to good communications is a failure to establish empathy between sender and receiver.
    II. The difference in status or rank between the sender and receiver of a communication may be a communications barrier.
    III. Communications are easier if they travel upward from subordinate to superior
    The choice below which MOST accurately describes the above statements is:
    A. I, II and III are incorrect.
    B. I and II are incorrect.
    C. I, II, and III are correct.
    D. I and II are correct.
    E. I and III are incorrect.

KEY (CORRECT ANSWERS)

1.	B		11.	C
2.	D		12.	A
3.	A		13.	C
4.	A		14.	C
5.	D		15.	C
6.	D		16.	C
7.	A		17.	D
8.	D		18.	A
9.	A		19.	D
10.	A		20.	C

21. A
22. A
23. E
24. D
25. E

READING COMPREHENSION
UNDERSTANDING AND INTERPRETING WRITTEN MATERIAL

EXAMINATION SECTION

TEST 1

DIRECTIONS: Each question or incomplete statement is followed by several suggested answers or completions. Select the one that BEST answers the question or completes the statement. *PRINT THE LETTER OF THE CORRECT ANSWER IN THE SPACE AT THE RIGHT.*

1. Most managers make the mistake of using absolutes as signals of trouble or its absence. A quality problem emerges—that means trouble; a test is passed—we have no problems. Outside of routine organizations, there are always going to be such signals of trouble or success, but they are not very meaningful. Many times everything looks good, but the roof is about to cave in because something no one thought about and for which there is no rule, procedure, or test has been neglected. The specifics of such problems cannot be predicted, but they are often signaled in advance by changes in the organizational system: Managers spend less time on the project; minor problems proliferate; friction in the relationships between adjacent work groups or departments increases; verbal progress reports become overly glib, or overly reticent; change occur in the rate at which certain events happen, not in whether or not they happen. And they are monitored by random probes into the organization—seeing how things are going.
According to the above paragraph,
   A. managers do not spend enough time managing
   B. managers have a tendency to become overly glib when writing reports
   C. managers should be aware that problems that exist in the organization may not exhibit predictable signals of trouble
   D. managers should attempt to alleviate friction in the relationship between adjacent work groups by monitoring random probes into the organization's problems

1.____

2. *Lack of challenge* and *excessive zeal* are opposite villains. You cannot do your best on a problem unless you are motivated. Professional problem solvers learn to be motivated somewhat by money and future work that may come their way if they succeed. However, challenge must be present for at least some of the time, or the process ceases to be rewarding. On the other hand, an excessive motivation to succeed, especially to succeed quickly, can inhibit the creative process. The tortoise-and-the-hare phenomenon is often apparent in problem solving. The person who thinks up the simple elegant solution, although he or she may take longer in doing so, often wins. As in the race, the tortoise depends upon an inconsistent performance from the rabbit. And if the rabbit spends so little time on conceptualization that the rabbit merely chooses the first answers that occur, such inconsistency is almost guaranteed.

2.____

According to the above paragraph,
- A. excessive motivation to succeed can be harmful in problem solving
- B. it is best to spend a long time on solving problems
- C. motivation is the most important component in problem solving
- D. choosing the first solution that occurs is a valid method of problem solving

3. Virginia Woolf's approach to the question of women and fiction, about which she wrote extensively, polemically, and in a profoundly feminist way, was grounded in a general theory of literature. She argued that the writer was the product of her or his historical circumstances and that material conditions were of crucial importance. Secondly, she claimed that these material circumstances had a profound effect on the psychological aspects of writing, and that they could be seen to influence the nature of the creative work itself. According to this paragraph,
   - A. the material conditions and historical circumstances in which male and female writers find themselves greatly influence their work
   - B. a woman must have an independent income to succeed as a writer
   - C. Virginia Woolf preferred the writings of female authors, as their experiences more clearly reflected hers
   - D. male writers are less likely than women writers to be influenced by material circumstances

3.____

4. A young person's first manager is likely to be the most influential person in his or her career. If this manager is unable or unwilling to develop the skills the young employee needs to perform effectively, the latter will set lower personal standards than he or she is capable of achieving, that person's self-image will be impaired, and he or she will develop negative attitudes toward the job, the employer—in all probability—his or her career. Since the chances of building a successful career with the employer will decline rapidly, he or she will leave, if that person has high aspirations, in hope of finding a better opportunity. If, on the other hand, the manager helps the employee to achieve maximum potential, he or she will build a foundation for a successful career. According to the above paragraph,
   - A. If an employee has negative attitudes towards his or her job, the manager is to blame
   - B. managers of young people often have a great influence upon their careers
   - C. good employees will leave a job they like if they are not given a chance to develop their skills
   - D. managers should develop the full potential of their young employees

4.____

5. The reason for these difference is not that the Greeks had a superior sense of form or an inferior imagination or joy in life, but that they thought differently. Perhaps an illustration will make this clear. With the historical plays of Shakespeare in mind, let the reader contemplate the only extant Greek play on a historical subject, the Persians of Aeschylus, a play written less than ten years after the event which it deals with, and performed before the Athenian people who had played so notable a part in the struggle—incidentally,

5.____

immediately below the Acropolis which the Persians had sacked and defiled. Any Elizabethan dramatist would have given us a panorama of the whole war, its moments of despair, hope, and triumph; we should see on the stage the leaders who planned and some of the soldiers who won the victory. In the Persians we see nothing of the sort. The scene is laid in the Persian capital, one action is seen only through Persian eyes, the course of the war is simplified so much that the naval battle of Artemisium is not mentioned, nor even the heroic defense of Thermopylae, and not a single Greek is mentioned by name. The contrast could hardly be more complete.
Which sentence is BEST supported by the above paragraph?
- A. Greek plays are more interesting than Elizabethan plays.
- B. Elizabethan dramatists were more talented than Greek dramatists.
- C. If early Greek dramatists had the same historical material as Shakespeare had, the final form the Greek work would take would be very different from the Elizabethan work.
- D. Greeks were historically more inaccurate than Elizabethans.

6. The problem with present planning systems, public or private, is that accountability is weak. Private planning systems in the global corporations operate on a set of narrow incentives that frustrate sensible public policies such as full employment, environmental protection, and price stability. Public planning is Olympian and confused because there is neither a clear consensus on social values nor political priorities. To accomplish anything, explicit choices must be made, but these choices can be made effectively only with the active participation of the people most directly involved. This, not nostalgia for small-town times gone forever, is the reason that devolution of political power to local communities is a political necessity. The power to plan locally is a precondition for sensible integration of cities, regions, and countries into the world economy.
According to the author,
    - A. people most directly affected by issues should participate in deciding those issues
    - B. private planning systems are preferable to public planning systems
    - C. there is no good system of government
    - D. county governments are more effective than state governments

6.____

Questions 7-11.

DIRECTIONS: Questions 7 through 11 are to be answered SOLELY on the basis of the following passage.

   The ideal relationship for the interview is one of mutual confidence. To try to pretend, to put on a front of cordiality and friendship is extremely unwise for the interviewer because he will certainly convey, by subtle means, his real feelings. It is the interviewer's responsibility to take the lead in establishing a relationship of mutual confidence.
   As the interviewer, you should help the interviewee to feel at ease and ready to talk. One of the best ways to do this is to be at ease yourself. If you are, it will probably be evident; if you are not, it will almost certainly be apparent to the interviewee. Begin the interview with topics for discussion which are easy to talk about and non-menacing. This interchange can be like the

conversation of people when they are waiting for a bus, at the ballgame, or discussing the weather. However, do not prolong this warm-up too long since the interviewee knows as well as you do that these are not the things he came to discuss. Delaying too long in betting down too business may suggest to him that you are reluctant to deal with the topic.

Once you get onto the main topics, do all that you can to get the interviewee to talk freely with a little prodding from you as possible. This will probably require that you give him some idea of the area and of ways of looking at it. Avoid, however, prejudicing or coloring his remarks by what you say; especially, do not in any way indicate that there are certain things you want to hear, others which you do not want to hear. It is essential that he feel free to express his own ideas unhampered by your ideas, your values and preconceptions.

Do not appear to dominate the interview, nor have even the suggestion of a patronizing attitude. Ask some questions which will enable the interviewee to take pride in his knowledge. Take the attitude that the interviewee sincerely wants the interview to achieve its purpose. This creates a warm, permissive atmosphere that is most important in all interviews.

7. Of the following, the BEST title for the above passage is
   A. PERMISSIVENESS IN INTERVIEWING
   B. INTERVIEW TECHNIQUES
   C. THE FACTOR OF PRETENSE IN THE INTERVIEW
   D. THE CORDIAL INTERVIEW

8. Which of the following recommendations on the conduct of an interview is made by the above passage?
   A. Conduct the interview as if it were an interchange between people discussing the weather.
   B. The interview should be conducted in a highly impersonal manner.
   C. Allow enough time for the interview so that the interviewee does not feel rushed.
   D. Start the interview with topics which are not threatening to the interviewee.

9. The above passage indicates that the interviewer should
   A. feel free to express his opinions
   B. patronize the interviewee and display a permissive attitude
   C. permit the interviewee to give the needed information in his own fashion
   D. provide for privacy when conducting the interview

10. The meaning of the word *unhampered*, as it is used in the last sentence of the fourth paragraph of the above passage, is MOST NEARLY
    A. unheeded   B. unobstructed   C. hindered   D. aided

11. It can be INFERRED from the above passage that
    A. interviewers, while generally mature, lack confidence
    B. certain methods in interviewing are more successful than others in obtaining information
    C. there is usually a reluctance on the part of interviewers to deal with unpleasant topics
    D. it is best for the interviewer not to waiver from the use of hard and fast rules when dealing with clients

Questions 12-19.

DIRECTIONS: Questions 12 through 19 are to be answered SOLELY on the basis of the following passage.

Disabled cars pose a great danger to bridge traffic at any time, but during rush hours it is especially important that such vehicles be promptly detected and removed. The term *disable car* is an all-inclusive label referring to cars stalled due to a flat tire, mechanical failure, an accident, or locked bumpers. Flat tires are the most common reason why cars become disabled. The presence of disabled vehicles caused 68% of all traffic accidents last year. Of these, 75% were serious enough to require hospitalization of at least one of the vehicle's occupants.

The basic problem in the removal of disabled vehicles is detection of the car. Several methods have been proposed to aid detection. At a 1980 meeting of traffic experts and engineers, the idea of sinking electronic eyes into roadways was first suggested. Such *eyes* let officers know when traffic falls below normal speed and becomes congested. The basic argument against this approach is the high cost of installation of these eyes. One Midwestern state has, since 1978, employed closed circuit television to detect the existence and locations of stalled vehicles. When stalled vehicles are seen on the closed circuit television screen, the information is immediately communicated by radio to units stationed along the roadway, thus enabling the prompt removal of these obstructions to traffic. However, many cities lack the necessary manpower and equipment to use this approach. For the past five years, several east-coast cities have used the method known as *safety chains*, consisting of mobile units which represent the links at the *safety chain*. These mobile units are stationed as posts one or two miles apart along roadways to detect disabled cars. Standard procedure is for the units in the *safety chain* to have roof blinker lights turned on to full rotation. The officer, upon spotting a disabled car, at once assumes a post that gives him the most control in directing traffic around the obstruction. Only after gaining such control does he investigate and decide what action should be taken.

12. From the above passage, The PERCENTAGE of accidents caused by disabled cars in which hospitalization was required by at least one of the occupants of a vehicle last year was
    A. 17%   B. 51%   C. 68%   D. 75%

13. According to the above passage, vehicles are MOST frequently disabled because of
    A. flat tires
    B. locked bumpers
    C. brake failure
    D. overheated motors

14. According to the above passage, in the electronic eye method of detection, the *eyes* are placed
    A. on lights along the roadway
    B. on patrol cars stationed along the roadway
    C. in booths spaced two miles apart
    D. into the roadway

15. According to the above passage, the factor COMMON to both the *safety chain* method and the *closed circuit television* method of detecting disabled vehicles is that both
    A. require the use of *electronic eyes*
    B. may be used where there is a shortage of officers
    C. employ units that are stationed along the highway
    D. require the use of trucks to move the heavy equipment used

15.____

16. The one of the following which is NOT discussed in the above passage as a method that may be used to detect disabled vehicles is
    A. closed circuit television
    B. radar
    C. electronic eyes
    D. safety chains

16.____

17. One DRAWBACK mentioned by the above passage to the use of the closed circuit television method for detection of disabled cars is that this technique
    A. cannot be used during bad weather
    B. does not provide for actual removal of the cars
    C. must be operated by a highly skilled staff of traffic engineers
    D. requires a large amount of manpower and equipment

17.____

18. The NEWEST of the methods discussed in the above passage for detection of disabled vehicles is
    A. electronic eyes
    B. the mobile unit
    C. the safety chain
    D. closed circuit television

18.____

19. When the *safety chain* method is being used, an officer who spots a disabled vehicle should FIRST
    A. turn off his roof blinker lights
    B. direct traffic around the disabled vehicle
    C. send a ratio message to the nearest mobile unit
    D. conduct an investigation

19.____

20. The universe is 15 billion years old, and the geological underpinnings of the earth were formed long before the first sea creature slithered out of the slime. But it is only in the last 6,000 years or so that men have descended into mines to chop and scratch at the earth's crust. Human history is, as Carl Sagan has put it, the equivalent of a few seconds in the 15 billion year life of the earth. What alarms those who keep track of the earth's crust is that since 1950 human beings have managed to consume more minerals than were mined in all previous history, a splurge of a millisecond in geologic time that cannot be long repeated without using up the finite riches of the earth.
Of the following, the MAIN idea of this paragraph is:
    A. There is true cause for concern at the escalating consumption of the earth's minerals in recent years.
    B. Human history is the equivalent of a few seconds in the 15 billion year life of the earth
    C. The earth will soon run out of vital mineral resources

20.____

21. The authors of the Economic Report of the President are collectively aware, despite their vision of the asset-rich household, of the real economy in which millions of Americans live. There are glimpses, throughout the Report, of the underworld in which about 23 million people do not have public or private health insurance; in which the number of people receiving unemployment compensation was 41 percent of the total unemployed, in which the average dole for the compensated unemployed is about one-half of take-home pay. The authors understand, for example, that a worker may become physically disabled and that individuals generally do not like the risk of losing their ability to earn income. But such realities justify no more than the most limited interference in the (imperfect) market for disability insurance. There is only, as far as I can tell, one moment of genuine emotion in the entire Report when the authors' passions are stirred beyond market principles. They are discussing the leasing provisions of the 1981 Tax Act (conditions which so reduce tax revenues that they are apparently opposed in their present form by the Business Roundtable, the American Business Conference, and the National Association of Manufacturers).

    In the dark days before the 1981 ACT, according to the Report, (*firms with temporary tax losses* (a condition especially characteristic of new enterprises) were often unable to take advantage of investment tax incentives. The reason was that temporarily unprofitable companies had no taxable income against which to apply the investment tax deduction. It was a piteous contingency for the truly needy entrepreneur. But all was made right with the Tax Act. Social Security for the disabled incompetent corporation: the compassionate soul of Reagan's new economy.

    According to the above passage,
    - A. the National Association of Manufacturers and those companies that are temporarily unprofitable oppose the leasing provisions of the 1981 Tax Act
    - B. the authors of the Report are willing to ignore market principles in order to assist corporations unable to take advantage of tax incentives
    - C. the authors of the Report feel the National Association of Manufacturers and the Business Roundtable are wrong in opposing the leasing provisions of the 1981 Tax Act
    - D. the authors of the Report have more compassion for incompetent corporations than for disabled workers

21.____

22. Much of the lore of management in the West regards ambiguity as a symptom of a variety of organizational ills whose cure is larger doses of rationality, specificity, and decisiveness. But is ambiguity sometimes desirable? Ambiguity may be thought of as a shroud of the unknown surrounding certain events. The Japanese have a word for it, *ma*, for which there is no English translation. The word is valuable because it gives an explicit place to the unknowable aspect of things. In English, we may refer to an empty space between the chair and the table; the Japanese don't say the space is empty but *full of nothing*. However amusing the illustration, it goes to the core of the issue. Westerners speak of what is unknown primarily in reference to what is known (like the space between the chair and the table, while most eastern languages give honor to the unknown in its own right.

22.____

Of course, there are many situations that a manager finds himself in where being explicit and decisive is not only helpful but necessary. There is considerable advantage, however, in having a dual frame of reference—recognizing the value of both the clear and the ambiguous. The point to bear in mind is that in certain situations, ambiguity may serve better than absolute clarity.

Which sentence is BEST supported by the above passage?
- A. We should cultivate the art of being ambiguous.
- B. Ambiguity may sometimes be an effective managerial tool,
- C. Westerners do not have a dual frame of reference.
- D. It is important to recognize the ambiguous aspects of all situations.

23. Everyone ought to accustom himself to grasp in his thought at the same time facts that are at once so few and so simple, that he shall never believe that he has knowledge of anything which he does not mentally behold with a distinctiveness equal to that of the objects which he knows most distinctly of all. It is true that some people are born with a much greater aptitude for such discernment than others, but the mind can be made much more expert at such work by art and exercise. But there is one fact which I should here emphasize above all others; and that is everyone should firmly persuade himself that none of the sciences, however abstruse, is to be deduced from lofty and obscure matters, but that they all proceed only from what is easy and more readily understood.

    According to the author,
    - A. people should concentrate primarily on simple facts
    - B. intellectually gifted people have a great advantage over others
    - C. even difficult material and theories proceed from what is readily understood
    - D. if a scientist cannot grasp a simple theory, he or she is destined to fail

23.____

24. Goethe's casual observations about language contain a profound truth. Every word in every language is a part of a system of thinking unlike any other. Speakers of different languages live in different worlds; or rather, they live in the same world but can't help looking at it in different ways. Words stand for patterns of experience. As one generation hand its language down to the next, it also hands down a fixed pattern of thinking, seeing, and feeling. When we go from one language to another, nothing stays put; different peoples carry different nerve patterns in their brains, and there's no point where they fully match.

    According to the above passage,
    - A. language differences and their ramifications are a major cause of tensions between nations
    - B. it is not a good use of one's time to read novels that have been translated from another language because of the tremendous differences in interpretation
    - C. differences in languages reflect the different experiences of people the world over
    - D. language students should be especially careful to retain awareness of the subtleties of their native language

24.____

Questions 25-27.

DIRECTIONS: Questions 25 through 27 are to be answered SOLELY on the basis of the following passage.

    The context of all education is twofold—individual and social. Its business is to make us more and more ourselves, too cultivate in each of us our own distinctive genius, however modest it may be, while showing us how this genius may be reconciled with the needs and claims of the society of which we are a part. Thought it is not education's aim to cultivate eccentrics, that society is richest, most flexible, and most humane that best uses and most tolerates eccentricity. Conformity beyond a point breeds sterile minds and, therefore, a sterile society.
    The function of secondary—and still more of higher education is to affect the environment. Teachers are not, and should not be, social reformers. But they should be the catalytic agents by means of which young minds are influenced to desire and execute reform. To aspire to better things is a logical and desirable part of mental and spiritual growth.

25. Of the following, the MOST suitable title for the above passage is 25.____
   A. EDUCATION'S FUNCTION IN CREATING INDIVIDUAL DIFFERENCES
   B. THE NEED FOR EDUCATION TO ACQUAINT US WITH OUR SOCIAL ENVIRONMENT
   C. THE RESPONSIBILITY OF EDUCATION TOWARD THE INDIVIDUAL AND SOCIETY
   D. THE ROLE OF EDUCATION IN EXPLAINIING THE NEEDS OF SOCIETY

26. On the basis of the above passage, it may be inferred that 26.____
   A. conformity is one of the forerunners of totalitarianism
   B. education should be designed to create at least a modest amount of genius in everyone
   C. tolerance of individual differences tends to give society opportunities for improvement
   D. reforms are usually initiated by people who are somewhat eccentric

27. On the basis of the above passage, it may be inferred that 27.____
   A. genius is likely to be accompanied by a desire for social reform
   B. nonconformity is an indication of the inquiring mind
   C. people who are not high school or college graduates are not able to affect the environment
   D. teachers may or may not be social reformers

Questions 28-30.

DIRECTIONS: Questions 28 through 30 are to be answered SOLELY on the basis of the following passage.

    Disregard for odds and complete confidence in one's self have produced many of our great successes. But every young man who wants to go into business for himself should appraise himself as a candidate for the one percent to survive. What has he to offer that is new or better? Has he special talents, special know-how, a new invention or service, or more capital than the average competitor? Has he the most important qualification of all, a willingness to work harder than anyone else? A man who is working for himself without limitation of hours or personal sacrifice can run circles around any operation that relies on paid help. But he must forget the eight-hour day, the forty-hour week, and the annual vacation. When he stops work, his income stops unless he hires a substitute. Most small operations have their busiest day on Saturday, and the owner uses Sunday to catch up on his correspondence, bookkeeping, inventorying, and maintenance chores. The successful self-employed man invariably works harder and worries more than the man on a salary. His wife and children make corresponding sacrifices of family unity and continuity; they never know whether their man will be home or in a mood to enjoy family activities.

28. The title that BEST expresses the ideas of the above passage is   28._____
    A. OVERCOMING OBSTACLES
    B. RUNNING ONE'S OWN BUSINESS
    C. HOW TO BECOME A SUCCESS
    D. WHY SMALL BUSINESSES FAIL

29. The above passage suggests that   29._____
    A. small businesses are the ones that last
    B. salaried workers are untrustworthy
    C. a willingness to work will overcome loss of income
    D. working for one's self may lead to success

30. The author of the above passage would MOST likely believe in   30._____
    A. individual initiative   B. socialism
    C. corporations   D. government aid to small business

KEY (CORRECT ANSWERS)

1.	C	11.	B	21.	D
2.	A	12.	B	22.	B
3.	A	13.	A	23.	C
4.	B	14.	D	24.	C
5.	C	15.	C	25.	C
6.	A	16.	B	26.	D
7.	B	17.	D	27.	D
8.	D	18.	A	28.	B
9.	C	19.	B	29.	D
10.	B	20.	A	30.	A

PREPARING WRITTEN MATERIAL

PARAGRAPH REARRANGEMENT
COMMENTARY

The sentences that follow are in scrambled order. You are to rearrange them in proper order and indicate the letter choice containing the correct answer at the space at the right.

Each group of sentences in this section is actually a paragraph presented in scrambled order. Each sentence in the group has a place in that paragraph; no sentence is to be left out. You are to read each group of sentences and decide upon the best order in which to put the sentences so as to form a well-organized paragraph.

The questions in this section measure the ability to solve a problem when all the facts relevant to its solution are not given.

More specifically, certain positions of responsibility and authority require the employee to discover connection between events sometimes, apparently, unrelated. In order to do this, the employee will find it necessary to correctly infer that unspecified events have probably occurred or are likely to occur. This ability becomes especially important when action must be taken on incomplete information.

Accordingly, these questions require competitors to choose among several suggested alternatives, each of which presents a different sequential arrangement of the events. Competitors must choose the MOST logical of the suggested sequences.

In order to do so, they may be required to draw on general knowledge to infer missing concepts or events that are essential to sequencing the given events. Competitors should be careful to infer only what is essential to the sequence. The plausibility of the wrong alternatives will always require the inclusion of unlikely events or of additional chains of events which are NOT essential to sequencing the given events.

It's very important to remember that you are looking for the best of the four possible choices, and that the best choice of all may not even be one of the answers you're given to choose from.

There is no one right way to solve these problems. Many people have found it helpful to first write out the order of the sentences, as they would have arranged them, on their scrap paper before looking at the possible answers. If their optimum answer is there, this can save them some time. If it isn't, this method can still give insight into solving the problem. Others find it most helpful to just go through each of the possible choices, contrasting each as they go along. You should use whatever method feels comfortable and works for you.

While most of these types of questions are not that difficult, we've added a higher percentage of the difficult type, just to give you more practice. Usually there are only one or two questions on this section that contain such subtle distinctions that you're unable to answer confidently. And you then may find yourself stuck deciding between two possible choices, neither of which you're sure about.

EXAMINATION SECTION
TEST 1

DIRECTIONS: Each group of sentences in this section is actually a paragraph presented in scrambled order. Each sentence in the group has a place in that paragraph; no sentence is to be left out. You are to read each group of sentences so as to form a well-organized paragraph. Before trying to answer the questions which follow each group of sentences, jot down the correct order of the sentences. Then answer each of the questions by printing the letter of the correct answer in the space at the right. Remember that you will receive credit only for answers marked.

P. The awards to Eugene O'Neill, William Faulkner, and Ernest Hemingway were welcomed by all.
Q. Thereafter, in 1938 Pearl Buck won the prize.
R. Three of the six times that the Nobel Prize for Literature has been given to Americans, the choice has been universally approved.
S. Now, the award has gone to John Steinbeck.
T. But, in 1930, the prize went to Sinclair Lewis.

1. Which sentence did you put second
   A. P   B. Q   C. R   D. S   E. T

2. Which sentence did you put after Sentence S?
   A. P
   B. Q
   C. R
   D. T
   E. None of the above. Sentence S is last.

3. Which sentence did you put before Sentence Q?
   A. P
   B. R
   C. S
   D. T
   E. None of the above. Sentence Q is first.

4. Which sentence did you put first?
   A. P   B. Q   C. R   D. S   E. T

5. Which sentence did you put last?
   A. P   B. Q   C. R   D. S   E. T

KEY (CORRECT ANSWERS)

1. A
2. E
3. D
4. C
5. D

TEST 2

DIRECTIONS: Each group of sentences in this section is actually a paragraph presented in scrambled order. Each sentence in the group has a place in that paragraph; no sentence is to be left out. You are to read each group of sentences so as to form a well-organized paragraph. Before trying to answer the questions which follow each group of sentences, jot down the correct order of the sentences. Then answer each of the questions by printing the letter of the correct answer in the space at the right. Remember that you will receive credit only for answers marked.

P. Five months before he died, Herman Melville finished BILLY BUDD.
Q. Had he survived, Melville could have made BILLY BUDD as memorable and lucid awork as MOBY DICK.
R. Now, Peter Jones has written and directed a motion picture based on BILLY BUDD.
S. Unhappily, the film is a failure.
T. Several years ago, Robert Smith and Thomas Johnson
U. dramatized the book and brought it to the stage.

1. Which sentence did you put before Sentence Q?   1._____

   A. P
   B. R
   C. S
   D. T
   E. None of the above. Sentence Q is first.

2. Which sentence did you put after Sentence T?   2._____

   A. P
   B. Q
   C. R
   D. S
   E. None of the above. Sentence T is last.

3. Which sentence did you put after Sentence R?   3._____

   A. P
   B. Q
   C. S
   D. T
   E. None of the above. Sentence R is last.

4. Which sentence did you put before Sentence P?   4._____

   A. Q
   B. R
   C. S
   D. T
   E. None of the above. Sentence P is first.

5. Which sentence did you put first?   5._____
   A. P   B. Q   C. R   D. S   E. T

KEY (CORRECT ANSWERS)

1. A
2. C
3. C
4. E
5. A

TEST 3

DIRECTIONS: Each group of sentences in this section is actually a paragraph presented in scrambled order. Each sentence in the group has a place in that paragraph; no sentence is to be left out. You are to read each group of sentences so as to form a well-organized paragraph. Before trying to answer the questions which follow each group of sentences, jot down the correct order of the sentences. Then answer each of the questions by printing the letter of the correct answer in the space at the right. Remember that you will receive credit only for answers marked.

P. This spirit must occasionally find a direct outlet.
Q. The spirit of our culture is latent violence.
R. Hob violence will do perfectly as an outlet, however, since one cannot lose therespect of one's neighbors while they, too, are burning automobiles.
S. One must work within the spirit of his culture.
T. Murder will not do as a direct outlet, since it loses the respect of one's neighbors.

1. Which sentence did you put after Sentence R?

   A. P
   B. Q
   C. S
   D. T
   E. None of the above. Sentence R is last.

2. Which sentence did you put first?

   A. P   B. Q   C. R   D. S   E. T

3. Which sentence did you put after Sentence P?

   A. Q
   B. R
   C. S
   D. T
   E. None of the above. Sentence P is last.

4. Which sentence did you put after Sentence Q?

   A. P
   B. R
   C. S
   D. T
   E. None of the above. Sentence Q is last.

5. Which sentence did you put after Sentence S?

   A. P
   B. Q
   C. R
   D. T
   E. None of the above. Sentence S is last.

KEY (CORRECT ANSWERS)

1. E
2. D
3. D
4. A
5. B

TEST 4

DIRECTIONS: Each group of sentences in this section is actually a paragraph presented in scrambled order. Each sentence in the group has a place in that paragraph; no sentence is to be left out. You are to read each group of sentences so as to form a well-organized paragraph. Before trying to answer the questions which follow each group of sentences, jot down the correct order of the sentences. Then answer each of the questions by printing the letter of the correct answer in the space at the right. Remember that you will receive credit only for answers marked.

P. A few years ago, Franz Schmidt was appointed Germany's Foreign Minister.
Q. He had a Nazi background and was disliked intensely by the opposition.
R. During these past years, however, Schmidt has silenced his critics and confounded the political prophets.
S. He had also not been successful as Minister of the Interior.
T. Schmidt had no particular qualifications for the position and several disadvantages.

1. Which sentence did you put first?

   A. P   B. Q   C. R   D. S   E. T

2. Which sentence did you put after Sentence S?

   A. P
   B. Q
   C. R
   D. T
   E. None of the above. Sentence S is last.

3. Which sentence did you put before Sentence Q?

   A. P
   B. R
   C. S
   D. T
   E. None of the above. Sentence Q is first.

4. Which sentence did you put after Sentence R?

   A. P
   B. Q
   C. S
   D. T
   E. None of the above. Sentence R is last.

5. Which sentence did you put before Sentence S?

   A. P
   B. Q
   C. R
   D. T
   E. None of the above. Sentence S is first.

KEY (CORRECT ANSWERS)

1. A
2. C
3. D
4. E
5. B

TEST 5

DIRECTIONS: Each group of sentences in this section is actually a paragraph presented in scrambled order. Each sentence in the group has a place in that paragraph; no sentence is to be left out. You are to read each group of sentences so as to form a well-organized paragraph. Before trying to answer the questions which follow each group of sentences, jot down the correct order of the sentences. Then answer each of the questions by printing the letter of the correct answer in the space at the right. Remember that you will receive credit only for answers marked.

- P. But business is a fairly irresponsible form of government, since it is restrained only by its self-interest.
- Q. Business, in other words, is the politics of production.
- R. We have, therefore, two governments, both necessary, but only one subject to the will of the electorate.
- S. From early colonial times, business activity has always tended to be a form of government.
- T. It is, too, authoritarian.

1. Which sentence did you put after Sentence Q?

    A. P
    B. R
    C. S
    D. T
    E. None of the above. Sentence Q is last.

2. Which sentence did you put after Sentence R?

    A. P
    B. Q
    C. S
    D. T
    E. None of the above. Sentence R is last.

3. Which sentence did you put first?

    A. P   B. Q   C. R   D. S   E. T

4. Which sentence did you put next to last?

    A. P   B. Q   C. R   D. S   E. T

5. Which sentence did you put after Sentence S?

    A. P
    B. Q
    C. R
    D. T
    E. None of the above. Sentence S is last.

KEY (CORRECT ANSWERS)

1. A
2. E
3. D
4. E
5. B

PREPARING WRITTEN MATERIAL
EXAMINATION SECTION
TEST 1

DIRECTIONS: Each question consists of a sentence which may or may not be an example of good English usage. Examine each sentence, considering grammar, punctuation, spelling, capitalization, and awkwardness. Then choose the correct statement about it from the four choices below it. If the English usage in the sentence given is better than any of the changes suggested in choices B, C, or D, pick choice A. (Do not pick a choice that will change the meaning of the sentence.) *PRINT THE LETTER OF THE CORRECT ANSWER IN THE SPACE AT THE RIGHT.*

1. We attended a staff conference on Wednesday the new safety and fire rules were discussed.
   A. This is an example of acceptable writing.
   B. The words "safety," "fire," and "rules" should begin with capital letters.
   C. There should be a comma after the word "Wednesday."
   D. There should be a period after the word "Wednesday" and the word "the" should begin with a capital letter.

   1.____

2. Neither the dictionary or the telephone directory could be found in the office library.
   A. This is an example of acceptable writing.
   B. The word "or" should be changed to "nor."
   C. The word "library" should be spelled "libery."
   D. The word "neither" should be changed to "either."

   2.____

3. The report would have been typed correctly if the typist could read the draft.
   A. This is an example of acceptable writing.
   B. The word "would" should be removed.
   C. The word "have" should be inserted after the word "could."
   D. The word "correctly" should be changed to "correct."

   3.____

4. The supervisor brought the reports and forms to an employees desk.
   A. This is an example of acceptable writing.
   B. The word "brought" should be changed to "took."
   C. There should be a comma after the word "reports" and a comma after the word "forms."
   D. The word "employees" should be spelled "employee's."

   4.____

5. It's important for all the office personnel to submit their vacation schedules on time.
   A. This is an example of acceptable writing.
   B. The word "It's" should be spelled "Its."
   C. The word "their" should be spelled "they're."
   D. The word "personnel" should be spelled "personal."

   5.____

6. The report, along with the accompanying documents, were submitted for review.
   A. This is an example of acceptable writing.
   B. The words "were submitted" should be changed to "was submitted."
   C. The word "accompanying" should be spelled "accompaning."
   D. The comma after the word "report" should be taken out.

7. If others must use your files, be certain that they understand how the system works, but insist that you do all the filing and refiling.
   A. This is an example of acceptable writing.
   B. There should be a period after the word "works," and the word "but" should start a new sentence.
   C. The words "filing" and "refiling" should be spelled "fileing" and "refileing."
   D. There should be a comma after the word "but."

8. The appeal was not considered because of its late arrival.
   A. This is an example of acceptable writing.
   B. The word "its" should be changed to "it's."
   C. The word "its" should be changed to "the."
   D. The words "late arrival" should be changed to "arrival late."

9. The letter must be read carefuly to determine under which subject it should be filed.
   A. This is an example of acceptable writing.
   B. The word "under" should be changed to "at."
   C. The word "determine" should be spelled "determin."
   D. The word "carefuly" should be spelled "carefully."

10. He showed potential as an office manager, but he lacked skill in delegating work.
    A. This is an example of acceptable writing.
    B. The word "delegating" should be spelled "delagating."
    C. The word "potential" should be spelled "potencial."
    D. The words "he lacked" should be changed to "was lacking."

KEY (CORRECT ANSWERS)

1.	D	6.	B
2.	B	7.	A
3.	C	8.	A
4.	D	9.	D
5.	A	10.	A

TEST 2

DIRECTIONS: Each question consists of a sentence which may or may not be an example of good English usage. Examine each sentence, considering grammar, punctuation, spelling, capitalization, and awkwardness. Then choose the correct statement about it from the four choices below it. If the English usage in the sentence given is better than any of the changes suggested in choices B, C, or D, pick choice A. (Do not pick a choice that will change the meaning of the sentence.) *PRINT THE LETTER OF THE CORRECT ANSWER IN THE SPACE AT THE RIGHT.*

1. The supervisor wants that all staff members report to the office at 9:00 A.M.   1.____
   A. This is an example of acceptable writing.
   B. The word "that" should be removed and the word "to" should be inserted after the word "members."
   C. There should be a comma after the word "wants" and a comma after the word "office."
   D. The word "wants" should be changed to "want" and the word "shall" should be inserted after the word "members."

2. Every morning the clerk opens the office mail and distributes it.   2.____
   A. This is an example of acceptable writing.
   B. The word "opens" should be changed to "open."
   C. The word "mail" should be changed to "letters."
   D. The word "it" should be changed to "them."

3. The secretary typed more fast on a desktop computer than on a laptop computer.   3.____
   A. This is an example of acceptable writing.
   B. The words "more fast" should be changed to "faster."
   C. There should be a comma after the words "desktop computer."
   D. The word "than" should be changed to "then."

4. The new stenographer needed a desk a computer, a chair and a blotter.   4.____
   A. This is an example of acceptable writing.
   B. The word "blotter" should be spelled "blodder."
   C. The word "stenographer" should begin with a capital letter.
   D. There should be a comma after the word "desk."

5. The recruiting officer said, "There are many different goverment jobs available."   5.____
   A. This is an example of acceptable writing.
   B. The word "There" should not be capitalized.
   C. The word "government" should be spelled "government."
   D. The comma after the word "said" should be removed.

6. He can recommend a mechanic whose work is reliable.   6.____
   A. This is an example of acceptable writing.
   B. The word "reliable" should be spelled "relyable."
   C. The word "whose" should be spelled "who's."
   D. The word "mechanic should be spelled "mecanic."

73

7. She typed quickly; like someone who had not a moment to lose.   7._____
   A. This is an example of acceptable writing.
   B. The word "not" should be removed.
   C. The semicolon should be changed to a comma.
   D. The word "quickly" should be placed before instead of after the word "typed."

8. She insisted that she had to much work to do.   8._____
   A. This is an example of acceptable writing.
   B. The word "insisted" should be spelled "incisted."
   C. The word "to" used in front of "much" should be spelled "too."
   D. The word "do" should be changed to "be done."

9. He excepted praise from his supervisor for a job well done.   9._____
   A. This is an example of acceptable writing.
   B. The word "excepted" should be spelled "accepted."
   C. The order of the words "well done" should be changed to "done well."
   D. There should be a comma after the word "supervisor."

10. What appears to be intentional errors in grammar occur several times in the passage.   10._____
    A. This is an example of acceptable writing.
    B. The word "occur" should be spelled "occurr."
    C. The word "appears" should be changed to "appear."
    D. The phrase "several times" should be changed to "from time to time."

KEY (CORRECT ANSWERS)

1.	B	6.	A
2.	A	7.	C
3.	B	8.	C
4.	D	9.	B
5.	C	10.	C

TEST 3

DIRECTIONS: Each question consists of a sentence which may or may not be an example of good English usage. Examine each sentence, considering grammar, punctuation, spelling, capitalization, and awkwardness. Then choose the correct statement about it from the four choices below it. If the English usage in the sentence given is better than any of the changes suggested in choices B, C, or D, pick choice A. (Do not pick a choice that will change the meaning of the sentence.) *PRINT THE LETTER OF THE CORRECT ANSWER IN THE SPACE AT THE RIGHT.*

1. The clerk could have completed the assignment on time if he knows where these materials were located.
    A. This is an example of acceptable writing.
    B. The word "knows" should be replaced by "had known."
    C. The word "were" should be replaced by "had been."
    D. The words "where these materials were located" should be replaced by "the location of these materials."

2. All employees should be given safety training. Not just those who accidents.
    A. This is an example of acceptable writing.
    B. The period after the word "training" should be changed to a colon.
    C. The period after the word "training" should be changed to a semicolon, and the first letter of the word "Not" should be changed to a small "n."
    D. The period after the word "training" should be changed to a comma, and the first letter of the word "Not" should be changed to a small "n."

3. This proposal is designed to promote employee awareness of the suggestion program, to encourage employee participation in the program, and to increase the number of suggestions submitted.
    A. This is an example of acceptable writing.
    B. The word "proposal" should be spelled "proposal."
    C. The words "to increase the number of suggestions submitted" should be changed to "an increase in the number of suggestions is expected."
    D. The word "promote" should be changed to "enhance" and the word "increase" should be changed to "add to."

4. The introduction of inovative managerial techniques should be preceded by careful analysis of the specific circumstances and conditions in each department.
    A. This is an example of acceptable writing.
    B. The word "technique" should be spelled "techneques."
    C. The word "inovative" should be spelled "innovative."
    D. A comma should be placed after the word "circumstances" and after the word "conditions."

5. This occurrence indicates that such criticism embarrasses him.
   A. This is an example of acceptable writing.
   B. The word "occurrence" should be spelled "occurence."
   C. The word "criticism" should be spelled "critisism."
   D. The word "embarrasses" should be spelled "embarasses."

KEY (CORRECT ANSWERS)

1. B
2. D
3. A
4. C
5. A

LIBRARY SCIENCE

TABLE OF CONTENTS

	Page
LIBARIES AND LIBRARIANSHIP	1
BACKGROUND	1
Introduction	1
History of Libraries	1
Growth of Libraries in the United States	1
Professionalization	2
FACETS AND SCOPE OF LIBRARIANSHIP	2
Demand for Libraries in the Economy	2
Public Libraries	2
School Libraries	2
College and University Libraries	3
Special Libraries	3
The Modern Library	3
OCCUPATIONAL DESCRIPTIONS	4
Acquisitions Librarian	4
Bookmobile Driver	4
Bookmobile Librarian	4
Cataloger	5
Chief Librarian	5
Children's Librarian	6
Classifier	6
Collector, Overdue Material	7
Field Librarian	7
Film Librarian	8
Librarian	8
Librarian, Special Collections	9
Librarian, Special Library	9
Library Assistant	10
Library Associate Director	10
Library Director	11
Page	11
Patients' Librarian	11
Registration Clerk	12
School Librarian	12
Shelving Supervisor	12
Young Adult Librarian	13

LIBRARY SCIENCE

LIBRARIES AND LIBRARIANSHIP

BACKGROUND

INTRODUCTION
In the history of man, the communication of ideas has been the factor which distinguishes him from the lower animals. The ability to pass on knowledge and culture through the medium of speech led to the growth of civilization. Just as important, however, was the development of a means of preserving knowledge through written records, for it is this accumulated wealth of information which has enabled man to control his environment and to uncover some of the mysteries of the earth and heavens.

Throughout recorded history, it has been the duty of the librarian to preserve and organize the books and other records which contain man's knowledge and ideas so that they may be used most effectively to further the growth of civilization.

HISTORY OF LIBRARIES
Libraries have existed ever since man has written. Ancient Egypt boasted collections of papyrus rolls, while the Babylonians and Assyrians gathered together their cuneiform covered clay tablets so that they could be cataloged and preserved. Undoubtedly, the two most famous libraries of the ancient world were at Alexandria. In the third century B.C., only a few years after their founding, the larger of the two was reported to contain over a half million papyrus rolls. Some of the earliest experiments in bibliography were the catalogs of the Alexandrian libraries.

It was in ancient Rome that public libraries flourished in abundance and that the science of librarianship became recognized. The first large book collections were acquired as the spoils of war. The Romans realized their importance and enlarged them, in addition to building library collections of their own. In the fourth century, Rome had twenty-eight public libraries. With the fall of the Empire, however, books were withdrawn to monasteries and private collections. Not until the advent of the printing press in the middle of the fifteenth century did books again become plentiful and libraries again grow.

GROWTH OF LIBRARIES IN THE UNITED STATES
There have been books and libraries in the United States since the early days of the Colonies. The first organized library was founded in 1638 at Harvard University. As other colleges were instituted in the Colonies, they too established libraries for the use of their faculties and students. Public libraries did not come as quickly. The nearest approach to public library service was the subscription library, the first being Benjamin Franklin's Library Company, organized in Philadelphia in 1731 The first public library in the United States to be directly established by state legislation was the Boston library. In1838, Massachusetts passed legislation specifically designed to allow the city of Boston to establish a public library and to appropriate municipal funds for its support. Earlier, Peterborough, New Hampshire, formed the first tax-supported library in 1833 on the basis of a state law passed in 1821 permitting a certain portion of tax revenue to be used for schools and other educational purposes

PROFESSIONALIZATION

The years between 1850 and 1870 saw a period of rapid growth. Not only were college and public libraries flourishing, but governmental and specialized libraries achieved importance; and as the prestige of libraries grew, so did the role of the librarian and his responsibility. Librarianship became a profession in its own right. Realizing that librarians needed an organization to help them to utilize more fully the available materials and to standardize procedures, Melvil Dewey and other prominent members of the profession called a nationwide meeting of librarians in 1876, and the American Library Association was founded. This was the first of many professional organizations which have arisen to meet the needs of librarians in the ever-widening fields of knowledge which they serve.

FACETS AND SCOPE OF LIBRARIANSHIP

DEMAND FOR LIBRARIANS IN THE ECONOMY

As the scope of man's knowledge has increased and as the numbers of his written works have grown, so have libraries and the need for librarians. At the first meeting of the American Library Association in 1876, only one hundred and four persons were present. At that time, there were approximately 1,000 librarians in the United States. It was estimated that there were more than 150,000 active professional librarians. Public libraries, colleges, and universities, schools, governmental agencies, public and private institutions, and commercial and industrial firms all have need of the librarian's services.

In general, it may be said that librarianship is a service profession, one in which the individual, no matter what his level of responsibility or specialization, devotes his time to satisfying the needs of others to obtain informational material. Because so many of the agencies, firms, and institutions cited above have realized the importance of having trained librarians administer to the needs of their staffs, faculties, students, or patrons, the demand for librarians continues to increase. According to the United States Department of Labor, the number of librarians is expected to increase by 4.9%, while library technicians increase by 13.4% and library assistants by 12.5% by 2014.

While the largest number of 2000 graduates (32%) were placed in college and university libraries, the need for librarians in many phases of activity can be seen from the fact that 29% of the graduates accepted positions in public libraries, 21% became school librarians, and 18% undertook special and other library work.

PUBLIC LIBRARIES

The public library in the United States today is a tax-supported institution, providing direct service to all members of the community. Informational, educational, and recreational materials are available, with special programs for work with children and young people, older persons, and adult education groups. The librarians involved in these programs must be knowledgeable as to the books and other materials available and the particular psychology of the age and social groups of the people whom they are serving.

SCHOOL LIBRARIES

The school library is established by the educational governing body, usually the Board of Education, in a school community to provide books and other educational materials to the children and faculties in the elementary and secondary schools. The librarian in a school library is usually required to have a background in educational theories as well as a degree in Library Science since he or she must provide supplementary teaching aids.

COLLEGE AND UNIVERSITY LIBRARIES
The college or university library, like the school library, is established to serve the particular community of an educational institution. Research materials are stressed. In the large universities, there may be several libraries, each one serving an individual college or department, i.e., the science library, medical school library, or art school library.

SPECIAL LIBRARIES
The field of special librarianship is widely diversified. In general, there are two types of special libraries: (1) The special organization library, serving all informational needs of an organization such as a corporation or governmental agency, in which both the staff and clientele are employees of the same organization; (2) the special subject library, which may be semi-public, independent, departmental, or branch library, serving students, professional groups, or members on a given subject. The special librarian must often be a specialist in a particular field of information. He must be aware of current publications and research, and be able to assemble, organize, and maintain this information so that it may be of greatest use to the library's clientele.

THE MODERN LIBRARY
The modern library, recognizing the many media of communication available today, includes a variety of materials in its collection. Not only are books and periodicals found on library shelves, but many institutions provide audio/video material, advanced media and internet access to patrons, along with the records, films, and slides that remain vital even in today's advanced technological age. A few public libraries have framed paintings and other pictures which may be borrowed. Braille and talking books for the blind are available, as are ceiling-protected books for the bedridden.

Modern methods are used to increase library efficiency. Microfilm and digital copies of magazines and newspapers are important space-savers, as well as effective means of preserving information. Various systems of photographic charging of materials have resulted in a saving of man-hours and an elimination of many errors.

One of the newest ways in which libraries are utilizing modern science is in the use of automatic data processing systems for library cataloging and documentation. The introduction of these new systems has been brought about by the fact that in the second half of the 20th century and into the new millennium, the production of information has accelerated with startling speed and intensity. Approximately 50% of all scholarly material available today has been produced in the last fifteen years; there are now approximately 50,000 technical journals being published, and the number is expected to increase at the rate of 1,000 yearly; in scientific areas, it has been estimated that up to 2 million articles are published yearly.

New theories are being developed and new techniques are being applied to handle this flow of information. Complex electronic and mechanical means of information storage and retrieval are being developed to organize, catalog, classify, and index the wide diversity of information.

It is in the special library, the research library, and in specialized areas of the public library where the greatest concentration of information control has taken place. A number of organizations have created large information exchange networks, spanning the continent. In the future, it is expected that countries around the world will participate in the operation of information exchange systems.

OCCUPATIONAL DESCRIPTIONS

ACQUISITIONS LIBRARIAN
0-23.10
(100.288)

OCCUPATIONAL DEFINITION
    Selects and orders books, periodicals, films, and other materials for library. Reviews publishers' announcements and catalogs, and compiles lists of publications to be purchased. Compares selections with card catalog and orders-in-process to avoid duplication. Circulates selection list to branches and departments for comments. Selects vendors on basis of such factors as discount allowances and delivery dates. Compiles statistics on purchases, such as total purchases, average price, and fund allocations. May recommend acquisition of materials from individuals or organizations or by exchange with other libraries. Collaborates daily with other units, with additional library staff, and with vendors and publishers to provide optimal access to library materials for the community. Will participate in providing materials budget estimates, establishing fund allocations, monitoring expenditures and fiscal closing.

EDUCATIONAL AND TRAINING REQUIREMENTS
Master's degree in Library Science. Training time, from 1 to 2 years.

BOOKMOBILE DRIVER
7-36.260
(109.368)

OCCUPATIOAL DEFINITION
    Drives bookmobile or light truck that pulls book trailer, and assists in providing library services in mobile library. Drives vehicle to specified locations on predetermined schedule. Places books and periodicals on shelves according to such groupings as subject matter, readers' age grouping, or reading level. Stamps dates on library cards, files cards, and collects fines. Compiles reports of mileage, number of books issued, and amount of fines collected. Drives vehicle to garage for repairs, such as motor or transmission overhauls, and for preventive maintenance, such as chassis lubrication and oil change. Charges and discharges library material, in a timely manner. Assists patrons in locating appropriate library materials. Responds to ready reference questions. Takes application and issues library cards.

EDUCATIONAL AND TRAINING REQUIREMENTS
Tenth grade or above. Training time, approximately two months.

BOOKMOBILE LIBRARIAN
0-23.20
(100.168)

OCCUPATIONAL DEFINITION
    Provides library services for mobile library within given geographical area: Surveys community needs, and selects books and other materials for library. Publicizes visits to

area to stimulate reading interest. May prepare special collections for schools and other groups. May arrange bookmobile schedule. May drive bookmobile. (This job is a specialization of LIBRARIAN and shares the same basic duties.)

EDUCATIONAL AND TRAINING REQUIREMENTS
Master's degree in Library Science. Training time, three months.

CATALOGER
0-23.10
(100.388)
Catalog librarian; descriptive cataloger.

OCCUPATIONAL DEFINITION
   Compiles information on library materials, such as books and periodicals, and prepares catalog cards to identify materials and to integrate information into library catalog: Verifies author, title, and classification number on sample catalog card received from CLASSIFIER against corresponding data on title page. Fills in additional information, such as publisher, date of publication, and edition. Examines material and notes additional information, such as bibliographies, illustrations, maps, and appendices. Copies classification number from sample card into library material for identification. Files card in assigned sections of catalog. Tabulates number of sample cards according to quantity of material and catalog subject headings to determine number of new cards to be ordered or reproduced. Prepares inventory cards to record purchase information and location of library material. Requisitions additional cards. Records new information, such as death date of author and revised edition date, to amend cataloged cards. May specialize in regularly issued publications such as journals, periodicals, and bulletins, and be known as Serials Cataloger. In some instances, depending on the needs of the particular library system, the duties of CATALOGER and CLASSIFIER are combined into one occupation given the title of CATALOGER.

EDUCATIONAL AND TRAINING REQUIREMENTS
Master's degree in Library Science. Training time, one year.

CHIEF LIBRARIAN – BRANCH OR DEPARTMENT
0-23.20
(100.168)

OCCUPATIONAL DEFINITION
   Supervises staff, coordinates activities of library branch or department, and assists patrons in selection and location of books, films, audio/video items, web applications, and other materials. Trains and assigns duties to workers. Directs workers in performance of such tasks as receiving, shelving, and locating materials. Examines book reviews, publishers' catalogs, and other information sources to recommend material acquisition. Supervises and directs the arrangement of materials on shelves or in files according to classification code, titles, or authors' names. Selects materials such as newspaper clippings and pictures to maintain special collections. Searches catalog files, biographical dictionaries, and indexes, and examines content of reference materials to assist patrons in locating and selecting materials. May assemble and arrange materials for display. May

prepare replies to mail requests for information. May compile lists of library materials and recommend materials to individuals or groups and be designated Readers'Advisory-Service Librarian. May be designated according to type of library as Chief Librarian, Branch; Chief Librarian, Bookmobile; or according to department as Chief Librarian, Art Department; Chief Librarian, Circulation Department; Chief Librarian, Music Department; Chief Librarian, Readers' Advisory Service.

EDUCATIONAL AND TRAINING REQUIREMENTS
Master's degree in Library Science. Training time of 2 to 4 years serving in various professional positions in a library system. Experience should reflect proven ability to supervise others.

CHILDREN'S LIBRARIAN
0-23.20
(100.168)

OCCUPATIONAL DEFINITION
   Assists children in selecting and locating library materials, and organizes and conducts activities for children to encourage reading and use of library facilities: Confers with teachers, parents, and community groups to relate library services to the concerns of adults working with children. Stimulates children's discriminate reading by organizing such activities as story hours, reading clubs, book fairs, and summer reading programs. Shows films, tell stories, and gives book talks to encourage reading. Conducts library tours to acquaint children with library facilities and services. (This job is a specialization of LIBRARIAN and shares the same basic duties.)

EUCATIONAL AND TRAINING REQUIREMENTS
Master's degree in Library Science. Training time, six months to one year.

CLASSIFIER
0-23.1
(100.388)
Subject cataloger

OCCUPATIONAL DEFINITION
   Classifies library materials such as books, films, audio/video material and periodicals according to subject matter: Reviews materials to be classified and searches information sources, such as book reviews, encyclopedias, online reference material and technical publications, to determine subject matter of materials.
   Selects classification numbers and descriptive headings according to Dewey Decimal, Library of Congress, or other library classification systems. Makes sample cards containing author, title, and classification number to guide CATALOGER in preparing catalog cards for books and periodicals. Assigns classification numbers, descriptive headings, and explanatory summaries to book and catalog cards to facilitate locating and obtaining materials. Composes annotations (explanatory summaries) of material content.

EDUCATIONAL AND TRAINING REQUIREMENTS
Master's degree in Library Science. Training time, from 1 to 4 years, depending on areas of responsibility, and size and complexity of library system.

COLLECTOR, OVERDUE MATERIAL
1-15.69
(240.368)

OCCUPATIONAL DEFINITION
Collects fines and overdue library material from borrowers: Sorts copies of overdue notices, according to street addresses, to plan collection route. Drives to address shown on overdue notice and explains purpose of call to borrower. Attempts to obtain overdue material and fine, or library card. Collects payment for lost material. Schedules return appointment to obtain material not on premises or advises borrower of alternative methods of returning materials. Records reasons for failure to collect material on overdue notice.

EDUCATIONAL AND TRAINING REQUIREMENTS
High school graduate. Training time, one week.

FIELD LIBRARIAN
0-23.01
(100.118)
Library consultant; state field consultant

OCCUPATIONAL DEFINITION
Advises administrators, members of trustee boards, and civic groups on matters designed to improve the organization, administration, and service of public libraries: Discusses personnel staffing patterns, building plans, and book collections with administrators who request consultation service from State. Analyzes administrative policies, observes work procedures, and reviews data relative to book collections to determine effectiveness of library service to public. Compares allotments designated for building funds, salaries, and book collections with standards prepared by State agencies, to determine effectiveness of budget. Gathers statistical data, such as population and community growth rates, and analyzes building plans to determine adequacy of programs for expansion. Prepares evaluation of library systems based on observations and surveys, and recommends measures to improve organization and administration of systems according to state program for libraries and professional experience. Presents surveys of salary standards, budget analyses, and tentative building programs to administrators as suggested means of improving administration of library systems. Negotiates with civic groups, boards of trustees, and library administrators who wish to consolidate library systems to resolve jurisdictional disputes and differences of opinion. Informs citizen groups of state legal requirements relative to library consolidations. Explains eligibility requirements for programs offering State and Federal financial assistance to libraries and recommends measures to be taken to attain eligibility and apply for aid. Plans and organizes programs for the recruitment of professional personnel. Directs the establishment of work procedures in new or reorganized library systems. Recommends methods of enlarging book collections. Plans and organizes training programs for administrators to inform them of recent developments in public administration and library

science. Addresses town meetings and civic organizations to explain programs offered by State Division of Libraries. Occasionally demonstrates or performs all professional and clerical tasks associated with public libraries.

EDUCATIONAL AND TRAINING REQUIREMENTS
Master's degree in Library Science. Approximately five years of experience in professional library work, with at least two years as administrator.

FILM LIBRARIAN
0-23.10
(100.168)
Audiovisual librarian; film-and-record librarian

OCCUPATIONAL DEFINITION
   Plans film programs and keeps library of film and other audio-visual materials: Reviews records/CDs and motion-picture soundtracks, and motion pictures, considering their technical, informational, and esthetic qualities, to select materials for library collection. Prepares brief summary of film content for catalog. Prepares and arranges film programs for presentation to groups. Advises those planning to install film program on technical problems, such as acoustics, lighting, and program content, and leads discussions after film showing. May maintain or oversee maintenance of audio and video material. Operates audio/visual equipment, film projectors, CD/DVD players, splicers, rewinders, and film-inspection equipment.

EDUCATIONAL AND TRAINING REQUIREMENTS
Master's degree in Library Science with additional training in film production techniques.

LIBRARIAN
0-23.20
(100.168)

OCCUPATIONAL DEFINITION
   Selects and maintains library collection of books, periodicals, documents, films, recordings, media technology and other materials, and assists groups and individuals to locate and obtain materials: Furnishes information on library activities, facilities, rules, and services. Explains use of reference sources, such as bibliographic indexes, reading guides, the internet and online applications to locate information. Describes or demonstrates procedures for searching catalog files, shelf collections and online and media applications to obtain materials. Searches catalog files and shelves to locate information. Issues and receives materials for circulation or for use in library. Assembles and arranges displays of books and other library materials. Performs variety of duties to maintain reference and circulation matter, such as copying author's name and title on catalog cards, and selecting and assembling pictures and newspaper clippings. Answers correspondence on special reference subjects. May compile book titles, bibliographies, or reading lists according to subject matter or designated interests to prepare reading lists. May select, order, catalog and classify materials. Librarians also compile lists of books, periodicals, articles, and audio-visual materials on particular subjects; analyze collections; and recommend materials. They collect and organize books, pamphlets, manuscripts, and

other materials in a specific field, such as rare books, genealogy, or music. In addition, they coordinate programs such as storytelling for children and literacy skills and book talks for adults, conduct classes, publicize services, provide reference help, write grants, and oversee other administrative matters. When engaged in locating information on specific subjects is known as Reference Librarian.

EDUCATIONAL AND TRAINING REQUIREMENTS
Master's degree in Library Science. Training time of six months to two years, depending on nature of assignment.

LIBRARIAN, SPECIAL COLLECTIONS
0-23.10
(100.168)

OCCUPATIONAL DEFINITION
　　Collects books, pamphlets, manuscripts, and rare newspapers, to provide source material for research: Organizes collections according to field of interest. Examines reference works and consults specialists preparatory to selecting materials for collections. Compiles bibliographies. Appraises subject materials, using references, such as bibliographies, book auction records, and special catalogs. Publishes papers and bibliographies on special collections to notify clientele of available materials. Lectures on booklore, such as history of printing, bindings, and illuminations. May plan and arrange displays for library exhibits. May index and reproduce materials for sale to other libraries. May specialize in rare books and be known as Rare Book Librarian.

EDUCATIONAL AND TRAINING REQUIREMENTS
Master's degree in Library Science. Training time may range up to five years, depending on complexity of field and size of collection.

LIBRARIAN, SPECIAL LIBRARY
0-23.20
(100.118)

OCCUPATIONAL DEFINITION
　　Manages library or section containing specialized materials for industrial, commercial, or governmental organizations, or for such institutions as schools and hospitals: Arranges special collections of technical books, periodicals, manufacturers' catalogs and specifications, film strips, motion pictures, CD/DVD and other media, and journal reprints. Searches literature, compiles accession lists, and annotates or abstracts materials. Assists patrons in research problems. May translate or order translation of materials from foreign languages into English. May be designated according to subject matter or specialty of library or department as Art Librarian; Business Librarian; Engineering Librarian; Law Librarian; Map Librarian; Medical Librarian.

EDUCATIONAL AND TRAINING REQUIREMENTS
Master's degree in Library Science. Training time, 1 to 2 years.

LIBRARY ASSISTANT
1-20.01
(100.368)

OCCUPATIONAL DEFINITION
Compiles records, sorts and shelves books, and issues and receives library materials, such as books, films, and CD-ROM: Records identifying data and due date on cards by hand or using photographic equipment to issue books to patrons. Inspects returned books for damage, verifies due date, and computes and receives overdue fines. Reviews records to compile list of overdue books and issues overdue notices to borrowers. Sorts books, publications, and other item according to classification code and returns them to shelves, files, or other designated storage area. Locates books and publications for patrons. Issues borrower's identification card according to established procedures. Files cards in catalog drawers according to system. Repairs books. Answers inquiries of nonprofessional nature on telephone and in person and refers persons requiring professional assistance to LIBRARIAN. May type material cards or issue cards and duty schedules. May be designated according to type of library as Bookmobile Clerk; Branch-Library Clerk; according to assigned department as Library Clerk, Art Department; or may be known according to tasks performed as Library Clerk, Book Return.

EDUCATIONAL AND TRAINING REQUIREMENTS
High school graduate. Training time, 6 to 12 months.

LIBRARY ASSOCIATE DIRECTOR
0-23.01
(100.118)

OCCUPATIONAL DEFINITION
Directs and assists with formulation and administration of library policies and procedures: Confers with department heads to coordinate reference services with technical processing and circulation activities. Meets with subordinate supervisory personnel to discuss goals and problems in library system. Observes functions in branch libraries to insure that established policies and work procedures are followed. Confers with LIBRARY DIRECTOR to discuss methods for increasing the efficiency of library service. Recommends reclassification of library jobs based on specific criteria of job evaluation, such as complexity of duties and scope of responsibility. Visits colleges, universities, and professional organizations to recruit workers. Forecasts growth of community from analysis of statistical data and plans building programs and expansion of library service into new areas. Acts for LIBRARY DIRECTOR in his absence.

EDUCATIONAL AND TRAINING REQUIREMENTS
Master's degree in Library Science. Training time, approximately 4 to 6 years, serving in various professional and supervisory positions in a library system.

LIBRARY DIRECTOR
0-23.01
(100.118)

OCCUPATIONAL DEFINITION
Plans and administers program of library services: Submits recommendations on library policies and services to governing body, such as board of directors or board of trustees, and implements policy decisions. Analyzes, selects, and executes recommendations of subordinates, such as department chiefs or branch supervisors. Analyzes and coordinates departmental budget estimates and controls expenditures to administer approved budget. Reviews and evaluates orders for books, film, and advanced media, examines trade publications and samples, interviews publishers' representatives, and consults with subordinates to select materials. Administers personnel regulations, interviews and appoints job applicants, rates staff performance, and promotes and discharges employees. Plans and conducts staff meetings and participates in community and professional committee meetings to discuss library problems. Delivers book reviews and lectures to publicize library activities and services. May examine and select materials to be discarded, repaired, or replaced. May be designated according to governmental subdivision served as City-Library Director; County-Library Director.

EDUCATIONAL AND TRAINING REQUIREMENTS
Master's degree in Library Science. Training time, approximately 4 to 8 years, serving in various professional and supervisory positions in a library system.

PAGE
1-23.14
(109.687)
Library page; runner; shelver; shelving clerk; stack clerk.

OCCUPATIONAL DEFINITION
Locates library materials such as books, periodicals, and pictures for loan, and replaces material in shelving area stacks) or files, according to identification number and title. Trucks or carries material between shelving area and issue desk. May cut premarked articles from periodicals.

EDUCATIONAL AND TRAINING REQUIREMENTS
Tenth to twelfth grade. Training time, from 1 to 3 months.

PATIENTS' LIBRARIAN
0-23.20
(100.168)
Hospital librarian.

OCCUPATIONAL DEFINITION
Analyzes reading needs of patients and provides library services for patients and employees in hospital or similar institution: Furnishes readers' advisory services on basis of knowledge of current reviews and bibliographies. Reviews requests, and selects books and other library materials for ward trips according to mental state, educational

background, and special needs of patients. Writes book reviews for hospital bulletins or newspapers and circulates reviews among patients. Provides handicapped or bedridden patients with reading aids, such as prism glasses, page turners, book stands, or talking books, and with other audio-visual material and aids. (This job is a specialization of LIBRARIAN and shares the same basic duties. See LIBRARIAN.)

EDUCATIONAL AND TRAINING REQUIREMENTS
Master's degree in Library Science. Training time, six months.

REGISTRATION CLERK
1-20.01
(109.368)

OCCUPATIONAL DEFINITION
Registers library patrons to permit them to borrow books, periodicals, and other library materials: Copies identifying data, such as name and address, from application onto registration list and borrowers' cards to register borrowers, and issues cards to borrowers. Records changes of address or name onto registration list and borrowers' cards to amend records.

EDUCATIONAL AND TRAINING REQUIREMENTS
High school graduate. Training time, 6 to 12 months.

SCHOOL LIBRARIAN
0-23.20
(100.168)

OCCUPATIONAL DEFINITION
Provides library service which includes book and audio-visual material selection, circulation, promotional work, reference, and general administration: Serves as a resource specialist for teachers, counselors, and other faculty members. Guides students in their reading and in use of communication media. (This job is a specialization of LIBRARIAN and shares the same basic duties. See LIBRARIAN.)

EDUCATIONAL AND TRAINING REQUIREMENTS
Master's degree in Library Science. Training time, 6 months to 2 years.

SHELVING SUPERVISOR
1-20.01
(109.138)

OCCUPATIONAL DEFINITION
Supervises and coordinates activities of library workers engaged in replacing books and other materials on shelves according to library classification system: Assigns duties to workers. Trains and directs workers in performance of shelving tasks. Examines materials on shelves to verify accuracy of placement. Counts number of materials placed

on shelves to record shelving activity. Marks designated classification number, subject matter, or title, to arrange material for shelving.

EDUCATIONAL AND TRAINING REQUIREMENTS
High school graduate. Training time, one year.

YOUNG ADULT LIBRARIAN
0-23.10
(100.288)

OCCUPATIONAL DEFINITION
    Directs young adult program in library to provide special activities for high school and college-age readers: Organizes young adults activities, such as chess clubs, creative writing club, and photography contests. Contacts speakers, writers, and distributes advertising, and meets young adult club representatives to prepare group programs. Delivers talks on books to stimulate reading. Addresses groups such as parent-teacher associations and civic organizations, to inform community of activities. Conducts high school classes on Library Tours to acquaint students with library facilities and services. Compiles lists of young adult reading materials for individuals, high school classes, and branch libraries. Issues and receives library materials, such as books and phonograph records. (This job is a specialization of LIBRARIAN and shares the same basic duties. See LIBRARIAN.)

EDUCATIONAL AND TRAINING REQUIREMENTS
Master's degree in Library Science with an additional one year training time.

BASIC FUNDAMENTALS OF LIBRARY SCIENCE

TABLE OF CONTENTS

	Page
DEWEY DECIMAL SYSTEM	1
PREPARING TO USE THE LIBRARY	1
THREE TYPES OF BOOK CARDS	2
Author Card	2
Title Card	2
Subject Card	3
Call Number	3
PERIODICALS	3
PERIODICALS FILE	3
PERIODICAL INDEXES	3
TEST IN LIBRARY SCIENCE	4
I. Using a Card Catalog	4
II. Understanding Entries in a Periodical Index	5
III. Identifying Library Terms	7
IV. Finding a Book by its Call Number	7
V. General	9
KEY (CORRECT ANSWERS)	10

BASIC FUNDAMENTALS OF LIBRARY SCIENCE

The problem of classifying' all human knowledge has produced a branch of learning called "library science." A lasting contribution to a simple and understandable method of locating a book on any topic was designed by Melvil Dewey in 1876. His plan divided all knowledge into ten large classes and then dubdivided each class according to related groups.

DEWEY DECIMAL SYSTEM

1. Subject Classification

The Dewey Decimal Classification System is the accepted and most widely used subject classification system in libraries throughout the world.

2. Classification by Three (3) Groups

There are three groups of classification in the system. A basic group of ten (10) classifications arranges all knowledge as represented by books within groups by classifications numbered 000-900.

The second group is the "100 division"; each group of the basic "10 divisions" is again divided into 9 sub-sctions allowing for more detailed and specialized subjects not identified in the 10 basic divisions.

3. There is a third, still further specialized "One thousand" group where each of the "100" classifications are further divided by decimalized, more specified, subject classifications. The "1,000" group is mainly used by highly specialized scientific and much diversified libraries.

These are the subject classes of the Dewey System:

000-099	General works (included bibliography, encyclopedias, collections, periodicals, newspapers,etc.)
100-199	Philosophy (includes psychology, logic, ethics, conduct, etc.) 200-299 Religion (includes mythology, natural theology, Bible, church history, etc.)
300-399	Social Science (includes economics, government, law, education, commerce, etc.)
400-499	Language (includes dictionaries, grammars, philology, etc.) 500-599 Science (includes mathematics, chemistry, physics, astronomy, geology, etc.) 600-699 Useful Arts (includes agriculture, engineering, aviation, medicine, manufactures, etc.) 700-799 Fine Arts (includes sculpture, painting, music, photography, gardening, etc.)
800-899	Literature (includes poetry, plays, orations, etc.) 900-999 History (includes geoegraphy, travel, biography, ancient and modern history, etc.)

PREPARING TO USE THE LIBRARY

Your ability to use the library and its resources is an important factor in determining your success. Skill and efficiency in finding the library materials you need for assignments and research papers will increase the amount of time you have to devote to reading or organizing information.

2

These are some of the preparations you can make now.
1. Develop skill in using your local library. You can increase your familiarity with the card catalog and the periodical indexes, such as the *Readers' Guide to Periodical Literature, in* any library.
2. Take the *Test in Library Science* to see how you can improve your knowledge of the library.
3. Read in such books as *Books, Libraries and You* by Jessie Edna Boyd, *The Library Key* by Margaret G. Cook, and *Making Books Work, a Guide to the Use of Libraries* by Jennie Maas Flexner.

You can find other titles by looking under the subject heading LIBRARIES AND READERS in the card catalog of your library. THREE TYPES OF BOOK CARDS

Here are the three general types of cards which are used to represent a book in the main catalog.

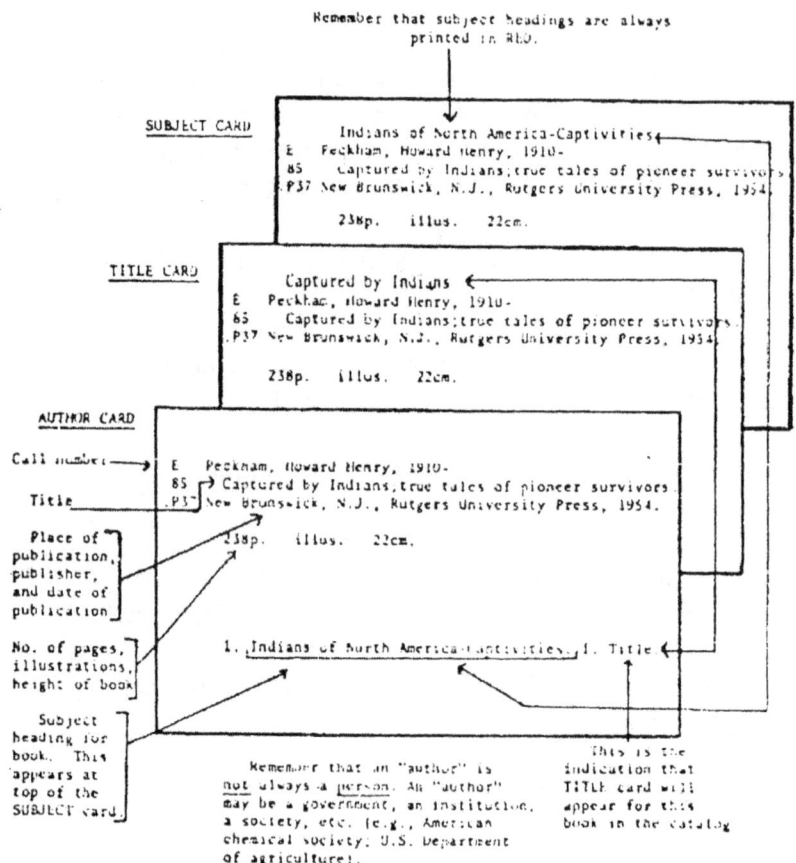

CARD CATALOG

The Card Catalog lists all books in the library by author. The majority of books also have title and subject cards.

Author card

If the author is known, look in the catalog under the author's name. The "author" for some works may be a society, an institution, or a government department.

Title card

Books with distinctive titles, anonymous works and periodicals will have a title card.

Subject card
To find books on a specific subject, look in the catalog under that subject heading. (Subject headings are printed in red on the Catalog Card.)

Call number
The letters and numbers in the upper left-hand corner of the Catalog Card are the book's call number. Copy this call number accurately, for it will determine the shelf location of the book. The word "Reference" marked in red in the upper right-hand corner of the catalog card indicates that the item is shelved in the Reference Section, and "Periodical "marked in yellow on the Catalog Card indicates that the item is shelved in the Periodicals Section. PERIODICALS

All magazines are arranged in alphabetical order by title. PERIODICALS FILE

To determine whether the Library has a specific magazine, consult the Periodicals File. Check the title of the magazine needed, and note that there are two cards for each title.

The bottom card lists the current issues available. The top card lists back bound volumes.

Those marked "Ask at Ref.Desk" may be obtained from the Reference Librarian. PERIODICAL INDEXES

Material in magazines is more up-to-date than books and is a valuable source of information. To find articles on a chosen subject, use the periodical indexes.

The Readers' Guide to Periodical Literature is the most familiar of these indexes. In the front of each volume is a list of the periodicals indexed and a key to abbreviations. Similar aids appear in the front of other periodical indexes.

Sample entry: WEASELS

        WONDERFUL WHITE WEASEL. R.Beck. il OUTDOOR LIFE 135:48-9+ Ja '65

Explanation :   An illustrated article on the subject WEASELS entitled WONDERFUL WHITE WEASEL, by R.Beck, will be found in volume 135 of OUTDOOR LIFE, pages 48-9 (continued on later pages of the same issue), the January 1965 number.

Major libraries subscribe to the following indexes:

Art Index
Biography Index
Book Review Index
British Humanities Index
Essay and General Literature Index
   This is helpful for locating criticism of works of literature.
An Index to Book Reviews in the Humanities
International Index ceased publications June, 1965 and continued as Social Science and Humanities Index
The Music Index The New York
Times Index Nineteenth Century Readers' Guide
Poole's Index
Poverty and Human Resources Abstracts
Psychological Abstracts
Public Affairs Information Service.Bulletin of the (PAIS) is a subject index to current books, pamphlets, periodical articles, government documents, and other library materials in economics and public affairs.

Readers' Guide to Periodical Literature
Social Science and Humanities Index a continuation of the International Index
Sociological Abstracts

Do you have the basic skills for using a library efficiently? You should be able to answer AT LEAST 33 of the following questions correctly. *CHECK YOUR ANSWERS BY TURNING TO THE ANSWER KEY AT THE BACK OF THIS SECTION.*
USING A CARD CATALOG
Questions 1-9.

DIRECTIONS: An author card (or "main entry" card) is shown below. Identify each item on the card by selecting the CORRECT letters for them. *PRINT THE LETTER OF THE CORRECT ANSWER IN THE SPACE AT THE RIGHT.*

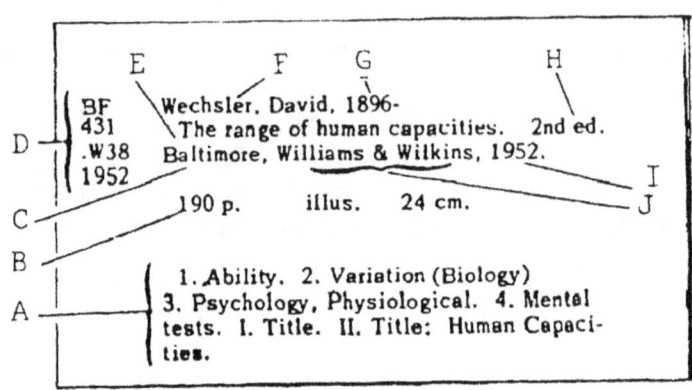

Sample Answer:

0. __F__

1. Date book was published. 1.__
2. Number of pages in book. 2.__
3. Title. 3.__
4. Place of publication. 4.__
5. Call number. 5.__
6. Year author was born 6.__
7. Edition. 7.__
8. Publisher. 8.__
9. Other headings under which cards for this book may be found. 9.__

Questions 10-13.

DIRECTIONS: Select the letter preceding the word or phrase which completes each of the following statements correctly.

10. The library's title card for the book THE LATE GEORGE APLEY can be found by looking in the card catalog under   10._____

    A. Apley, George   B. The   C. Late   D. George   E. Apley

11. A catalog card for a book by John F. Kennedy would be found in the drawer labelled   11._____

    A. JEFFERSON-JOHNSON,ROY
    B. PRESCOTT-PRICELESS
    C. KIERNAN-KLAY
    D. U.S.PRESIDENT-U.S.SOCIAL SECURITY
    E. KENNEBEC-KIERKEGAARD

12. The title cards for these three periodicals would be found in the card catalog arranged in which of the following orders: 12._____

    A. NEW YORKER, NEWSWEEK, NEW YORK TIMES MAGAZINE
    B. NEWSWEEK, NEW YORKER, NEW YORK TIMES MAGAZINE
    C. NEW YORK TIMES MAGAZINE, NEW YORKER, NEWSWEEK
    D. NEW YORKER, NEW YORK TIMES MAGAZINE, NEWSWEEK
    E. NEWSWEEK, NEW YORK TIMES MAGAZINE, NEW YORKER

13. A card for a copy of the U.N.Charter would be found in the catalog drawer marked   13._____

    A. TWENTIETH-UNAMUNO
    B. UNITED MINE WORKERS-UNITED SHOE MACHINERY
    C. U.S.BUREAU-U.S. CONGRESS
    D. U.S.SOCIAL POLICY-UNIVERSITAS
    E. CHANCEL-CIARDI

II. UNDERSTANDING ENTRIES IN A PERIODICAL INDEX

Questions 14-25.

DIRECTIONS: The following items are excerpts from THE READERS' GUIDE TO PERIODICAL LITERATURE. Identify each lettered section of the entries by placing the correct letters in the spaces.(There are more letters than spaces, so some of the letters will not be used.)

```
A ──── UNITED NATIONS                V
            Ambassador Goldberg holds news conference at         H ──── Security Council
            New York; transcript of conference,                         Security Council urged to respond to
B           July 28, 1965; with questions and answers.        U         challenge in southeast Asia; letter,
            A. J. Goldberg. Dept. State Bul 53:272+            M ── July 30, 1965. A. J. Goldberg. Dept
C ──── Ag 16 '65                                           T            State Bul 53:278-80+ Ag 16, '65
            U.N. out of its teens. I.D. Talmadge. il Sr Schol ── S        │     │  │
E ──── 87:16-17+  S 16 '65                                              L    •I  J  K
D ──── Whatever became of the United Nations?              Q
            America 113:235  S 4 '65
              F     R
                         Charter ──────────── P
            Up-dating the pre-atomic United Nations; address,
            June 20, 1965. C.P. Romulo. Vital Speeches
            31:658-61 Ag 15 '65; Excerpts. Sat R 48:34-5+
            Jl 24 '65 ─────────            O
                      N
                      G
```

14. Title of magazine containing a transcript of a news con-conference held by U.N. Ambassador Arthur Goldberg. 14.____

15. Magazine in which the full text of C.P. Romulo's address on the U.N. appears. 15.____

16. Author of an article titled U.N. OUT OF ITS TEENS. 16.____

17. Date on which Ambassador Goldberg wrote a letter urging the Security Council to respond to the challenge of southeast Asia. 17.____

18. Title of an article for which no author is listed. 18.____

19. Date of the SATURDAY REVIEW issue which contains excerpts of a speech called "Up-Dating the Pre-Atomic United Nations." 19.____

20. Pages in the DEPARTMENT OF STATE BULLETIN on which Ambassador Goldberg's letter appears. 20.____

21. Symbol indicating that the letter is continued on a later page. 21.____

22. Volume number of the magazine in which the article by I.D. Talmadge is printed. 22.____

23. Symbols meaning September 16, 1965. 23.____

24. The general subject heading under which all five articles are listed. 24.____

25. A subject heading subdivision. 25.____

Questions 26-27.

DIRECTIONS: Select the letter preceding the phrase which completes each of the following statements correctly.

26. To determine whether or not the library has THE MAGAZINE OF AMERICAN HISTORY, check in 26.____

   A. the list of magazine titles in the front of THE READERS' GUIDE TO PERIODICAL LITERATURE
   B. the library's card catalog

C. Ulrich's GUIDE TO PERIODICALS
D. SATURDAY REVIEW
E. THE LIBRARY JOURNAL

27. THE READERS' GUIDE is a good place to look for material on the Job Corps because it   27.____
    A. indexes only the best books and magazines in each field
    B. is a guide to articles on many subjects appearing in all of the library's periodicals
    C. indexes recent discussions on the subject in many magazines
    D. specializes in official government information
    E. does all of the above

III. IDENTIFYING LIBRARY TERMS

Questions 28-32.

DIRECTIONS: Match the correct definitions with these terms by placing the correct letters in the blanks. (Some of the letters will not be used.)

28.	Bibliography	A.	Word or phrase printed in A. Word or phrase printed in log to indicate the major log to indicate the major	28.____
29.	Anthology	B.	Brief written summary of the major ideas presented in an article or book	29.____
30.	Index	C.	List of books and/or articles on one subject or by one author	30.____
31.	Abstract	D.	Collection of selections from the writings of one or several authors	31.____
32.	Subject heading	E.	Written account of a person's life	32.____
		F.	Alphabetical list of subjects with the pages on which they are to be found in a book or periodical	
		G.	Subordinate, usually explanatory title, additional to the main title and usually printed below it	

IV. FINDING A BOOK BY ITS CALL NUMBER

Questions 33-38.

DIRECTIONS: The Library of Congress classification system call numbers shown below are arranged in order, just as the books bearing those call numbers would be arranged on the shelves. To show where other call numbers would be located, select the letter of the CORRECT ANSWER.

A.	B.	C.	D.	E.	F.	G.	H.	I.	J.	K.
PS 201 .L67 1961	PS 201 .M44	PS 208 .B87 1944	PS 351 .D7	PS 351 .D77	PS 3513 .A2	PS 3515 .D72	PS 3515.3 A66	PS 3526 .N21	PS 3526.17 P2	PS 3526.37 A10

L.	M.	N.
PS 3526.37 C20	PS 3526.37 C37	PT 1 .R2

33. A book with the call number PS
    201
    .L67
    would be shelved

   A. Before A   B. Between A & B   C. Between B & C
   D. Between C & D   E. Between D & E

34. A book with the call number PS
    208
    .B87
    1944a
    would be shelved

   A. Between A & B   B. Between C & D   C. Between B & C
   D. Between C & D   E. Between D & E

35. A book with the call number PS
    351
    D8
    would be shelved

   A. Between C & D   B. Between D & E   C. Between E & F
   D. Between F & G   E. Between G & H

36. A book with the call number PS
    3526.3
    M53
    would be shelved

   A. Between L & M   B. Between J & K   C. Between K & L
   D. Between M & O   E. Between O & P

37. A book with the call number PS
    3526.37
    C205
    would be shelved

   A. Between L & M   B. Between N & O   C. Between M & N
   D. Between O & P   E. Between P & Q

38. A book with the call number PS
    3526.37
    C3
    would be shelved

   A. Between M & N   B. Between L & M   C. Between N & O
   D. Between O & P   E. Between P & Q

V. General

Questions 39-40.

DIRECTIONS: Each question or incomplete statement is followed by several suggested answers or completions. Select the one that BEST answers the question or completes the statement. *PRINT THE LETTER OF THE CORRECT ANSWER IN TEE SPACE AT THE RIGHT.*

39. When it is finished (in 610 volumes), the _____ will be the MOST monumental national bibliography in the world. 39._____

 A. UNION LIST OF SERIALS IN LIBRARIES OF THE UNITED STATES AND CANADA
 B. UNITED STATES CATALOG
 C. READERS' GUIDE TO PERIODICAL LITERATURE
 D. NATIONAL UNION CATALOG

40. For those who wish to investigate the publishing companies and the people who control them, to locate the date a company was founded, who owned it, when it changed hands, what firm succeeded it, and other information of a similar nature, the periodical _____ is clearly invaluable. 40._____

 A. PUBLISHERS' TRADE LIST ANNUAL (PTLA)
 B. CUMULATIVE BOOK INDEX
 C. AMERICAN BOOKTRADE DIRECTORY
 D. PUBLISHERS WEEKLY

KEY (CORRECT ANSWERS)

1. I
2. B
3. E
4. C
5. D
6. G
7. H
8. J
9. A
10. C - The first word of the title which is not an article.
11. E - Every book in the library is listed in the card catalog under the author's name. (Warning: The "author" may be a society, a university, or some other institution.)
12. C - A title is alphabetized word-by-word; therefore, "New" comes before "Newsweek," "New York" before "New Yorker."
13. B - The United Nations, not an individual, is the author of this work.
14. T 16. Q 18. D 20. J 22. E 24. A 26. B 28. C 30. F 32. A
15. 0 17. M 19. N 21. K 23. R 25. P/H 27. C 29. D 31. B
33. A - When two call numbers are identical except that one has a year or some other figure added at its end, the shorter call numbers comes first.
34. B
35. C - The numbers which follow a. are regarded as decimals; therefore, .D77 precedes .D8.
36. B - 3526.3 precedes 3526.37
37. A - .C20 precedes .C205
38. B - .C3 precedes .C37 (Read the call number line-by-line, and put a J before a P, before a PB, etc. Put a lower number before a greater one.)
39. D
40. D